The Complete Plant-Based Diet Cookbook for Beginners

The Complete Plant-Based Diet Cookbook for Beginners

1000 Days Easy and Fresh Whole Food Plant-Based Recipes with 21 Days Meal Plan for Busy People

Carol Miller

CONTENT

Introduction

There has been extensive scientific research conducted in the past thirty years, on how different diets affect specific health issues, and our general health. Overwhelming evidence suggests that of all the different diets one can adopt, plant-based eating patterns are among the healthiest. A lot of recent nutrition research has examined plant-based eating patterns, and researchers have found these diets to have amazing health benefits. For example, the Mediterranean diet, which has a foundation of plant-based foods; but also includes fish, poultry, eggs, cheese, and yogurt, a few times a week, with meats and sweets much less often is frequently cited as one of the healthiest ways to eat. Exclusively plant-based diets – those with no animal products at all - have also been shown to support general health, and like the Mediterranean diet, can lower the risk of people developing coronary heart disease, high blood pressure, diabetes, while increasing longevity.

Plant-based diets, as the name suggests, focus on foods which are sourced primarily from plants. These include not only fruits and vegetables, but also nuts, seeds, whole grains, legumes, and beans. On this type of diet, you are simply going to be choosing more of your foods from plant sources than from any other. It's that easy!

A plant-based diet offers you all the necessary protein, fats, carbohydrates, vitamins, and minerals that your body needs for optimal health, and it is also higher in fiber and phytonutrients than a diet which contain more animal protein. A plant-based diet can be just as varied and interesting as any other diet. In short, it's going to be what you make of it!

I was not always an overweight person. I was lean and fit. But due to bad dietary choices, and a lack of regular exercise I eventually became so overweight that my health really suffered. I was a slim, sporty and energetic teenager, and when I was in my twenties, I still played a lot of sports, and I was always outdoors and on the go. I mostly walked everywhere. But, by the time I was in my thirties and forties I had gained a lot of excess fat and lost a lot of muscle tone.

Lifestyle changes, such as having a family to care for, and taking on a more sedentary job, meant that I got less formal and incidental exercise. I was also taking short-cuts with food, just to help me to fit all my commitments into each and every day. Eventually, my blood pressure and cholesterol levels were sky-high and my doctor warned me that I was a candidate for heart disease and Type 2 diabetes, if I did not make some radical changes to my eating patterns and exercise regime immediately. So, I took his good advice and I stared to make those essential lifestyle and dietary changes.

Obviously, the high-sugar, high-fat, processed and fast foods, that I relied upon because I thought they were more convenient, simply had to go. That was a no-brainer. So, I had to start all over again at the beginning, learning about nutrition, as I replaced those unhealthy foods with healthy fresh foods. One of the most important things that I learned right away was that I did not need to eat meat. I learned that I could create seriously tasty, nutritious meals, for myself and for my family, by using primarily plant-based foods. The eventual transition to a totally plant-based diet happened for me when I began to lose all that excess fat, and I started to feel so much healthier and more energetic again. I found that I naturally began to look out for healthy foods when I shopped, and when I cooked at home, I was also more aware of what I was putting into my family's meals, and into their growing bodies. Good nutrition should start in childhood!

Now, I want to share my new approach to cooking and eating in this cookbook. I want to show you how to sustain a healthy eating pattern that you find inspiring, creative and diverse. I want to share how to cook food at home that is exciting, appealing to all the family, and above all, good for your body. Most importantly, I want to show you that eating this way is not limiting, and that you won't be sacrificing taste and satisfaction by eating a plant-based diet!

As a species, humans eat only about 200 of the 300,000 edible plants on this planet. Yet, for some unfathomable reason, some people think that a plant-based diet lacks diversity and variety! This book is not a rigid regime or meal-planner. So, you probably want to know what's in the book? This book is a combination of recipes that will encourage you to appreciate what you are cooking and eating, and to be as creative as you can be when you prepare the food that sustains you, and encouragement to embrace changes. There is a little of everything in this book: from sweets and savories, to side dishes and condiments; appetizers and entrees that will make your mealtimes more interesting and exciting.

The techniques we show you in the book, to prepare the recipes, are not complicated, and the recipes themselves are super-easy to follow. In addition, none of the ingredients you will need is expensive or difficult to source. There is so much variety! We give you exotic dishes inspired by eastern flavours, and all those classic comfort foods that you grew up loving. There are sides, and garnished to enhance the meals too. The ingredients that you will be using are things that you have easy access to year-round, so the fun, creative part comes into play with the spices, seasonings, plants and textures that these recipes combine, to create an amazing variety of dishes for you to enjoy every day. The recipes in our cook book open up a world of flavour, and help you to make plant-based eating easy and appeal for all the family. Soon you will be cooking with confidence, and eating healthier than ever. And you won't even miss the junk food and unhealthy damaging foods that you probably eat without knowing how much damage they are doing to you! But first, some essential information.

What is a Plant-Based Diet?

You can choose to eat a plant-based diet in any of the following ways:

1.Semi-vegetarian or flexitarian.

This diet is probably the most common one, and it includes eggs, dairy foods, and sometimes meat, poultry, fish and seafood.

2.Pescatarian.

This diet includes eggs, dairy foods, fish and seafood, but it excludes meat and poultry completely.

3.Vegetarian.

This diet is becoming much more common. It includes eggs and dairy, but it excludes all meats, poultry and seafood completely.

4.Vegan.

Probably the most radical of the diets, but growing in popularity. In this diet, no animal foods are consumed at all. No eggs or dairy. Only vegetables, nuts, fruits, pulses and legumes are eaten.

The Benefits of a Plant-Based Diet

A plant-based diet supports your immune system. Plants hold essential nutrients that you cannot get from other foods. The vitamins and minerals, phytochemicals and antioxidants in plants help to keep your cells healthy and your body in balance. Therefore, your immune system can function at its best! Plants give your body what it needs to help fight off infection, and a plant-based diet will help to protect you against germs and harmful microorganisms.

Plant foods reduce inflammation. Plants' essential nutrients help resolve inflammation in your body. The same phytochemicals and antioxidants that boost your immune system, also travel around your body neutralizing toxins from pollution, processed food, harmful bacteria and viruses. Prolonged inflammation can damage your body's cells and tissue, and has been linked to cancer and other inflammatory diseases like arthritis. A plant-based diet may protect you because it helps to remove some of the triggers to these diseases.

A plant-based diet helps maintain a healthy weight. Sticking at a healthy weight is one of the most important things you can do to reduce your risk for cancer. Excess weight causes inflammation and hormonal imbalance. If you are overweight or obese, your overall risk is higher for twelve different types of cancer including colorectal, post-menopausal breast, uterine, esophageal, kidney and pancreatic.

Plants are high in fiber. Fiber is present in all unprocessed plant foods. It is what makes up the structure of the plant, so, if you eat more of it, you access a whole range of dietary benefits. Fiber can lower cholesterol and stabilize blood sugar. Plus, it's essential for good bowel management.

A plant-based diet reduces your risk for other diseases too. The benefits of eating mostly plants are not limited to reducing your cancer risk. A plant-based diet also has been shown to reduce your risk for heart disease, stroke, diabetes and some mental health illnesses.

What to Eat and Avoid Eating on a Plant-Based Diet

The Plant-Based Foods You Should Enjoy

To help get you get started, here's exactly what you can eat, as well as the things you might want to avoid on a plant-based diet. Most foods can fit into a plant-based diet. What's more important than the specific plant foods you're eating, is that you're eating plant foods at every meal. Aim to have some of your protein and healthy fat sources be plant-based. Pistachios, or a sliver of avocado, is ideal at snack time.

Vegetables

Non-starchy vegetables are low in calories but they boast both water and fiber, which help keep you fuller for longer. There are so many ways to use them, too. You can add grilled veggies to a salad, to create a "vegan power bowl", or make a white bean pizza, with tomatoes, and herbs.

- Broccoli
- Carrots
- Spinach
- Cabbage
- Kale
- Lettuce

Whole Grains

Whole grains are also excellent foods. Combined with non-starchy vegetables they deliver a serious energy-punch!

- Oats
- Millet
- Corn
- Brown rice
- Bulgur wheat
- Farro

Nuts

Another healthy plant-based fat source is nuts of all kinds. Almonds, cashews, walnuts - they're all good. Almost 90% of the fat found in pistachios, for instance, are mono and polyunsaturated fats. And, they have one of the highest contents of protein and fiber. Try using the following nuts in the recipes in this book.

- Almonds
- Pistachios
- Cashews
- Walnuts
- Pecans

Seeds

Like nuts, seeds are a simple way to add healthy fats, protein, and plenty of fiber to your diet. Even better, seeds can help fight off heart disease, keep your weight down, and prevent the accumulation of LDL cholesterol. And even though they're tiny, they're mighty: They contain high levels of omega-3 fatty acids, vitamins, and minerals that can help better your health and well-being. They also add crunch and texture to breads, cakes, salads and cookies!

- Quinoa
- Pumpkin seeds
- Hemp seeds
- Flax seeds
- Chia seeds
- Sunflower seeds
- Sesame seeds
- Poppy seeds

Legumes

So, where do plant-based eaters get most of their protein from, you ask? Legumes, which include beans, peas, and lentils. They're low in fat, contain zero cholesterol (unlike animal-based protein!), and they are loaded with fiber and

protein.

They are versatile, too. You can make veggie burgers with them, toss them into soups and stews, purée them into dips, or use them as a topping. Just pick up some legumes at the store and you'll quickly uncover an endless amount of delicious ways to prepare them with the help of this book.

- Chickpeas
- Peanuts
- Alfalfa
- Lentils
- Lentils
- Beans
- Clover

Beans

Okay, okay, beans are technically a legume! But, since there are so many of them, they're worthy of their own section among the best plant-based foods. Beans contain an impressive amount of fiber, protein, and vitamins and minerals, including zinc, iron, and magnesium. They're also great at keeping your heart and digestive system healthy and they are loaded with antioxidants, which can you help fight off disease. This cook book has scrummy recipes for the following types of beans.

- Black beans
- Fava beans
- Navy beans
- Edamame
- Kidney beans
- Pinto beans

- Soybeans

Spices

Eating plain broccoli might sometimes be a little boring, so that's what spices are for! When you're eating plant-based, having a pantry filled with options can completely transform your meals. Spices and herbs not only help to jazz up your meal, adding extremely few calories and no extra sugar, they also supply incredible health benefits. Ginger, for example, can help alleviate nausea and it also contains the substances gingerol and shogaol, which may help control inflammation in your body. Turmeric is another spice that's helpful for health, because it offers the polyphenol curcumin. It can actually help control knee pain as effectively as ibuprofen! Use these fabulous spices in our recipes and see for yourself!

- Ginger
- Turmeric
- Cinnamon
- Nutmeg
- Cumin
- Cumin
- Paprika
- Cloves
- Vanilla

Herbs

Like spices, using different herbs can also give your meals an upgrade in record time. They're also big on health benefits. Aside from adding great flavor, oregano has anti-cancer properties, and basil has been found to help strengthen the immune system, alleviate anxiety, and enhance memory. All that, and they are yummy! Supercharge your food with these herbs.

- Parsley
- Oregano
- Sage
- Rosemary
- Basil
- Thyme
- Chives
- Mint

Oil-Free Cooking and Foods Containing Healthy Fats

This cookbook contains recipes that do not use fats in the cooking process. You can substitute vegetable or fruit purée as a means of cooking sweet and savoury dishes without fats, and oven-baking on a non-stick paper or silicon sheet will prevent foods from sticking, without using oil. Not to say that all oils are bad, avocados, for example, contain heart-healthy fats and they also offer potassium - a mineral that can counteract sodium to help control your blood pressure levels, the oil in the avocado has the same properties as the flesh of the fruit. Try using some of the following foods that contain healthy oils and fats. Ground nuts can also be a great substitute for flour in some recipes.

- Olives
- Sesame seeds
- Hemp seeds
- Ground peanuts
- Avocados
- Flaxseeds
- Ground walnuts

The Plant-Based Foods You Should Avoid

There are some "baddies" in the plant-based world of food too, though. And you should either avoid them altogether, or limit them to very occasional treats. They won't do your health any favors. So, leave these bad boys out of your fridge and pantry.

Foods with added sugars

The amount of added sugar that manufacturing companies sneak into products is astonishing, I bet that you didn't know that most adults in the USA consume 10%, or more, of their daily calories from added sugar? Added sugar should be avoided as much as possible, so get your sugar buzz from natural sources like fruit instead. The following should not be part of your daily diet.

- Sable sugar
- Juices
- Ice cream
- Sodas
- Flavored yogurts

Artificial Sweeteners

Table sugar isn't allowed on a plant-based diet, and neither are artificial sweeteners. Instead, get your sugar from whole food sources like bananas, dates, or honey. It's also a very good idea to avoid all types of sugars and refined carbohydrates. Artificial sweeteners such as SPLENDA causes our taste buds in the feeding

centers of the brain to crave constant sweetness. Because of that, we're more likely to eat foods that contain simple carbohydrates or even to eat more food than we need just to satisfy that sweet-craving. None of these appear in our recipes.

- Splenda
- Sweet 'N Low
- Equal

Refined grains

While refined grains like white pasta and bread certainly qualify as plant-based foods, experts don't recommend them on the diet. And you won't find them in our cook book. Because they're stripped of the bran and germ in production, most of the nutrients and fiber are lost, And, because of that, they'll not only leave you hungry, they will also spike your blood sugar. Whole grains, on the other hand, have all of their nutrients and fiber intact, giving you a healthy, hearty, and satisfying carbohydrates to enjoy with your meals. That's why we include them in our cook book recipes. So, it's thumbs down to the following:

- White bread
- White tortillas
- White rice
- White pasta
- White flour

Packaged convenience foods

A plant-based diet definitely doesn't include packed foods! Unlike the vibrant whole foods that will make up the bulk of your diet when you cook our recipes, these non-nutritious foods are processed, and absolutely loaded with artificial colors and flavors, high amounts of sugar and sodium, and chemical additives. Yuk! Eating processed packaged convenience foods regularly can even increase your risk of heart disease, diabetes, and obesity. So, give them up and cook fresh. Your body won't miss any of this junk.

- Chips
- Frozen dinners
- Cereal
- Cookies
- Pizza

Processed meat

You've probably heard the not-so-flattering rumours about processed meat, and I am horrified to say that they are definitely true! Cutting back on processed red meat - such as hot dogs and sausage - is only going to benefit your health. Eating processed red meat is directly connected with a higher risk of colorectal cancer. Interestingly, eating plants can help negate the bad effects of red meat. The resistant starches in pulses can help reduce the risk of colon cancer that comes from a diet high in red meat. So, ditch the dogs, swerve the salami and banish the bacon!

- Salami
- Bacon
- Sausage
- Beef jerky

Processed plant-based foods

Of course, animal products should not be allowed on a plant-based diet, but all plant-based or vegan versions are okay, right? Not so fast! Processed packaged foods are total no-nos. Even though options free of animal products are often healthier and are made with healthier ingredients, they are just not wholesome enough for a plant-based diet. And that is why it's always a better idea to make your own homemade lentil or bean burger, for instance, as opposed to buying one at the store. The following are so processed that they just won't do your body any good.

- Soy-based frozen veggie burgers
- Faux meats
- Vegan eggs
- Vegan cheese
- Vegan frozen dinners

Processed cheese

I am sorry to be the bearer of bad news, but you are going to have to say goodbye to processed dairy cheese. It is simply loaded with saturated

fat, and eating it regularly can increase the amount of cholesterol in your blood, putting you at risk of heart disease. While vegan cheeses don't contain cholesterol, because they are not made with animal products, they are still not allowed on a plant-based diet, because they are so highly processed. So, I am sorry, but it is best if you say "ciao" to cheese.

- Dairy cheese
- Vegan cheese

Tips and Tricks

Following any new eating regime requires a little dedication and trial and error. But there are some things that you can do to make the transition easier and help you to shift seamlessly into a new routine and mind-set. Here are eight simple ways to kick-start a plant-based diet.

- Eat lots of veggies! Fill your plate with vegetables. Make sure you include a lot of variety, and eat them as a snack, with hummus or veggie/bean dips and salsa.
- Avoid all kinds of meats as much as possible.
- Choose good fats: nuts, seeds…all good choices. All low in cholesterol.
- Build meals around vegetables, whole grains and beans. This is kind of the whole point of the diet!
- Include whole grains for breakfast – to keep you energized and full. So, you won't be craving unhealthy snacks between breakfast and lunch.
- Go for greens! Kale, chard, spinach - they are all awesome! All packed with vitamins.
- Make a meal of salad – add herbs, beans, tofu, peas and vegetables. Sala is not just a side dish.
- Eat fruit for dessert instead of cakes and ice creams – watermelon, apples, grapes, pears, bananas… the choice is endless. Full of fiber, and delicious.

Frequently Asked Questions

You are bound to have a lot of questions about eating an exclusively whole-foods, plant-based diet. So, I've tried to capture as many of them as I can and I hope that my answers encourage you to explore more information and research.

Why is a whole-foods, plant-based diet good for me?

It will make you look and feel amazing! Plus, it will effectively help prevent and reverse chronic diseases. It will also give you loads of energy, and, as a bonus, if you've been carrying around some extra body fat, you'll find that it begins to just melt away. Since the 1970s, extensive nutrition research studies have shown that eating a whole-foods, plant-based diet is the key to optimum health.

Why should I avoid processed foods?

Eating a whole-foods, plant-based diet means avoiding refined foods such as white rice and bread. Basically, it avoids anything that has been through a process, is created artificially or has chemical additives. Whole foods are exactly that, foods that come from whole, unrefined plants. Any food that has been through a process has been stripped of most of its nutritional properties. This means that the good parts, such as healthy fiber, vitamins and minerals, have all been extracted. So, why would you want to eat something that nutritionally does not do anything good for you?

Is this diet going to be too restrictive?

There are so many different types of foods to eat on this diet. It could be said that you're restricting your diet if you only ever eat meat, poultry, fish and dairy. Right? It is very easy to eat meat-free, and by following the tips and tricks, you're going to be able to do that very quickly.

Will I need to take vitamin and mineral supplements?

Everybody is different: what they eat and their genetic make-up dictate their dietary needs. Generally, if you need to take a supplement it is probably because you have either a health issue, or a poor diet. Even vegetarians and vegans can have bad diets. For instance, people who rely on supermarket ready meals and takeaways are not getting correct nutrition, whether it is vegetarian processed food or not. Taking a vitamin or mineral supplement will not let you escape your health issue, or your bad diet. If you eat a healthy whole-food, plant-based diet, then you will more than likely be taking on board all the vitamins and minerals that you need. The only exceptions will be vitamin B12 and perhaps vitamin D, the sunshine vitamin. If you live in the northern hemisphere, you may need a supplement, particularly during the winter time.

Will I get enough protein on a plant-based diet?

How much protein do you think you need? 10%, 20%, 50% of your total calorie intake? Well, I will clarify this for you: the recommended daily allowance (RDA) for protein is 8-10% of total calories consumed. Unfortunately, there is a popular myth that you need animal protein. In fact, it can be harmful to us, and it can promote undesirable growth in our bodies, such as cancer cells and atherogenic tissue (essentially when the artery wall thickens as a result of the accumulation of fatty materials such as cholesterol and triglyceride). Eating plant proteins are better for us. So, don't worry about not getting enough protein, as long as you eat a varied vegetarian diet you will be healthy. Plant foods that contain protein include: grain foods such as bread, cereal, pasta and rice, nuts, beans and tofu.

Will I get enough calcium in my diet?

Another misconception is that plant-based diets are low in calcium. Vegetarian diets are actually packed full of calcium. You can get lots of calcium from green, leafy vegetables such as spinach, kale, and broccoli. Calcium is also found in dried figs, sesame seeds, tahini, beans, soybeans, and tofu.

Is it safe for children or pregnant women to follow a plant-based diet?

As long as you follow a healthy diet, with all the necessary amounts of calories, protein, vitamins and minerals for a growing body, then you will be absolutely fine.

Am I going to get fat? Aren't carbs bad for you?

This is one myth that I would like to debunk forever! Some people think that the sugars in starches are very easily converted into fat, and they think that they are carrying that extra fat because they eat too many starches. When we eat complex carbohydrates, our body breaks them down into simple sugars. Once broken down, these simple sugars are transported around our bodies in our blood stream, to trillions of cells, to provide them with energy. So, activity is the key to weight maintenance, not quitting carbs.

Now you have all the information you need to get started, literally, at your fingertips, it's time to go shopping for some wholesome plant-based foods, and start cooking with these easy-to-prepare recipes. Healthy eating can be fun!

Chapter 1 Basics

Oil-Free Hummus

Prep time: 10 minutes | Cook time: 0 minutes | Makes about 2 cups

1 (15-ounce / 425-g) can chickpeas, undrained
4 garlic cloves
¾ teaspoon ground cumin
½ teaspoon salt (optional)
¼ cup raw sesame seeds
Juice from ½ lemon
¼ teaspoon paprika

1. Put the chickpeas and about half of the liquid from the can in a blender or food processor. Add the sesame seeds, garlic, lemon juice, cumin, paprika, and salt (if using). Blend until creamy. Store in the refrigerator for up to 3 days.

Per Serving

Calories: 40 | fat: 2g | protein: 2g | carbs: 4g | fiber: 1g

Pure Nut Mylk

Prep time: 2 minutes | Cook time: 0 minutes | Makes 3 cups

1 cup raw, unsalted nuts (almonds, hazelnuts, Brazil nuts, pecans, macadamias, walnuts)
3 cups purified water for blending, plus more if desired

1. Soak the nuts overnight in 2 to 3 cups of water. 2. Drain and discard the soaking water and rinse the nuts well. Place the nuts in a blender along with the 3 cups of purified water. Blend on high speed for 2 to 3 minutes, or until smooth. 3. Strain the blended nut mixture through a cheesecloth or a nut milk bag, squeezing out as much liquid as possible. 4. If you want a thinner nut mylk, add more purified water as desired. 5. Pour into a glass jar and refrigerate. The mylk will keep in the refrigerator for 3 to 4 days.

Per Serving

Calories: 276 | fat: 23g | protein: 10g | carbs: 10g | fiber: 6g

Tahini Dressing

Prep time: 5 minutes | Cook time: 0 minutes | Makes ½ cup

¼ cup tahini
3 tablespoons lemon juice
1 teaspoon soy sauce
1 tablespoon olive oil (optional)
Pinch of salt and pepper (optional)
1 teaspoon minced garlic
1 tablespoon maple syrup (optional)
1 teaspoon ground cumin
1 tablespoon hot water

1. In a small bowl, whisk together all the ingredients until well combined. 2. Store in an airtight container in the fridge for up to 7 days.

Per Serving (½ cup)

Calories: 283 | fat: 24g | protein: 6g | carbs: 16g | fiber: 3g

Tofu Sour Cream

Prep time: 5 minutes | Cook time: 0 minutes | Makes 1½ cups

1 (12-ounce / 340-g) package extra-firm silken tofu, drained
Salt, to taste (optional)
1 tablespoon fresh lemon juice
1 tablespoon red wine vinegar

Combine all ingredients in a blender and purée until smooth and creamy. Chill until ready to serve.

Per Serving (½ cup)

Calories: 105 | fat: 6g | protein: 11g | carbs: 2g | fiber: 0g

Superfood Salad Topper

Prep time: 5 minutes | Cook time: 0 minutes | Makes 2⅓ cups

½ cup raw cashews
1 cup mixed seeds (sunflower, chia, flax, and hemp)
1 teaspoon curry powder
1 teaspoon ground turmeric
Pinch of cayenne pepper
½ cup sprouted or raw pumpkin seeds
⅓ cup goji berries
2 tablespoons flax oil or extra-virgin olive oil (optional)
½ teaspoon ground cinnamon
Pinch of sea salt (optional)

1. In a large bowl, combine the nuts, seeds and goji berries and toss with the oil (if using), curry powder, turmeric, cinnamon, cayenne and salt (if using). 2. Ideally, allow the mix to marinate for 15 minutes before serving. 3. Store the mixture in an airtight glass container in the fridge or freezer. It will keep fresh for weeks, ready to quickly nourish your meals.

Per Serving

Calories: 308 | fat: 27g | protein: 10g | carbs: 10g | fiber: 3g

Chili Powder

Prep time: 15 minutes | Cook time: 0 minutes | Makes about ½ cup

3 arbol chiles
5 California chiles
2 tablespoons garlic powder
1 tablespoon onion powder
5 guajillo chiles
2 tablespoons cumin seeds (not ground)
1 tablespoon dried oregano

1. Heat a cast-iron skillet over high heat. As the skillet heats up, remove and discard the stems and seeds from the arbol, guajillo, and California chiles. 2. Place the chiles in the hot, dry skillet and roast for 3 to 5 minutes, turning occasionally, until the color slightly changes and the chiles become softer. Transfer the chiles to a blender or food processor. 3. Put the cumin seeds in the hot skillet and toast until they begin popping. Immediately transfer them to the blender, along with the garlic powder, oregano, and onion powder. 4. Cover tightly and blend into a fine powder. Allow the powder to settle for 2 to 3 minutes before removing the lid. Store in a cool, dry location for up to 6 months.

Per Serving

Calories: 7 | fat: 0g | protein: 0g | carbs: 1g | fiber: 0g

Cheesy Sprinkle

Prep time: 5 minutes | Cook time: 0 minutes | Makes ½ cup

½ cup ground sunflower seeds, or Brazil nuts, or macadamia nuts
1 to 2 tablespoons nutritional yeast
2 teaspoons sea salt (optional)
1 tablespoon olive oil (optional)

1. Place the sunflower seeds in a small bowl, then add the salt (if using) and nutritional yeast. Mix to combine. 2. Leave as is for a dry sprinkle, or add just enough olive oil (if using) to bring the mixture together into a crumbly texture.

Per Serving (1 tablespoon)

Calories: 284 | fat: 25g | protein: 9g | carbs: 9g | fiber: 4g

Piecrust

Prep time: 10 minutes | Cook time: 0 minutes | Serves 4

1 cup all-purpose flour, plus more for rolling
¼ teaspoon salt (optional)
½ teaspoon lemon juice
3½ tablespoons plant-based milk
½ teaspoon baking powder
2 tablespoons canola oil, plus more if storing dough for later (optional)
4 tablespoons water

1. In a medium bowl, thoroughly mix all the ingredients with a wooden spoon until a ball of dough forms. 2. Wrap the dough in plastic wrap and refrigerate for 1 hour. 3. If using right away, dust a work surface with flour, place the chilled dough down, and roll it out into a thin, flat 11-inch circle using a lightly floured rolling pin. Transfer to a 9-inch pie dish. Fill with your choice of fillings and bake according to the recipe's instructions. 4. If not using right away, cover the exterior of the dough with 1 teaspoon oil or less (if desired) to keep it from drying out. Place this lightly oiled ball of dough in a medium bowl and cover tightly with plastic wrap (or place the dough in an airtight container). Refrigerate for up to 7 days.

Per Serving

Calories: 183 | fat: 8g | protein: 4g | carbs: 25g | fiber: 1g

Plant-Based Parmesan

Prep time: 5 minutes | Cook time: 0 minutes | Makes 1 heaping cup

1 cup raw cashews
¾ teaspoon garlic powder
⅓ cup nutritional yeast
½ teaspoon salt (optional)

1. In a blender or food processor, combine the cashews, nutritional yeast, garlic powder, and salt (if using). 2. Blend on medium-high until the mixture has the texture of grated parmesan cheese. You may need to stop and start the blender or food processor a couple of times to make sure the nuts are not clumping together on the bottom. Store in a glass or plastic container in the refrigerator for up to 1 month.

Per Serving

Calories: 219 | fat: 15g | protein: 11g | carbs: 14g | fiber: 4g

Creamy Avocado-Lime Dressing

Prep time: 5 minutes | Cook time: 0 minutes | Serves 6

1 avocado, diced
¼ cup cilantro leaves
¼ teaspoon salt (optional)
¼ cup fresh lime or lemon juice
½ teaspoon ground cumin
½ cup water, plus more as needed

1. Process all the ingredients in a high-speed blender until smooth. Adjust the seasoning and add the water, 1 tablespoon at a time, plus more as needed to achieve the desired consistency. Use within 1 day.

Per Serving

Calories: 57 | fat: 5g | protein: 1g | carbs: 4g | fiber: 2g

Maple-Dijon Dressing

Prep time: 5 minutes | Cook time: 0 minutes | Serves 4

¼ cup apple cider vinegar
2 teaspoons gluten-free Dijon mustard
2 tablespoons water
2 tablespoons maple syrup
¼ teaspoon black pepper
Salt (optional)

1. Combine the vinegar, maple syrup (if desired), mustard, pepper and water in a small jar with a tight-fitting lid. Season with salt to taste, if desired. Refrigerate for up to 5 days.

Per Serving

Calories: 31 | fat: 0g | protein: 0g | carbs: 7g | fiber: 0g

Cauliflower Béchamel

Prep time: 15 minutes | Cook time: 30 minutes | Makes about 3½ cups

1 large head cauliflower, cut into florets (about 3 cups)
2 cloves garlic, peeled and minced
¼ cup finely chopped basil
¼ teaspoon ground nutmeg
Unsweetened plain almond milk, as needed
1 medium yellow onion, peeled and diced small
2 teaspoons minced thyme
¼ cup nutritional yeast (optional)
Salt and freshly ground black pepper, to taste

1. Add the cauliflower to a large pot and add water to cover. Bring to a boil over high heat and cook until the cauliflower is very tender, about 10 minutes. Drain the excess water and purée the cauliflower using an immersion blender or in a blender with a tight-fitting lid, covered with a towel, in batches if necessary. Add almond milk, if needed, to achieve a creamy consistency. Set the purée aside while you prepare the rest of the ingredients. 2. Place the onion in a large skillet or saucepan and sauté over medium heat for 10 minutes. Add water 1 to 2 tablespoons at a time to keep the onion from sticking to the pan. Add the garlic, thyme, and basil and cook for another minute. Add the nutritional yeast (if using), nutmeg, and salt and pepper and cook for 5 minutes, or until heated through. 3. Add the onion mixture to the cauliflower purée and blend until smooth, adding up to ½ cup of water if necessary to achieve a smooth consistency.

Per Serving (½ cup)

Calories: 38 | fat: 0g | protein: 3g | carbs: 6g | fiber: 3g

Roasted Red Pepper Sauce

Prep time: 10 minutes | Cook time: 0 minutes | Makes 2 cups

1 (12-ounce / 340-g) package extra-firm silken tofu, drained
2 tablespoons chopped dill
½ teaspoon freshly ground black pepper
2 large red bell peppers, roasted and seeded
3 cloves garlic, peeled and chopped
1 teaspoon salt (optional)
Zest of 1 lemon

1. Combine all ingredients in the bowl of a food processor and purée until smooth and creamy. Refrigerate in an airtight container until ready to use.

Per Serving (1 cup)

Calories: 205 | fat: 11g | protein: 19g | carbs: 14g | fiber: 3g

Buckwheat Sesame Milk

Prep time: 5 minutes | Cook time: 0 minutes | Makes 4 cups

1 cup cooked buckwheat
1 teaspoon pure vanilla extract (optional)
3 cups water
1 tablespoon tahini, or other nut or seed butter
2 to 3 dates, or 15 drops pure stevia (or vanilla stevia), or 2 to 3 tablespoons unrefined sugar (optional)

1. Put everything in a blender, and purée until smooth. 2. Strain the fiber through a piece of cheesecloth or a fine-mesh sieve. 3. Keep in an airtight container in the fridge for up to 5 days.

Per Serving (1 cup)

Calories: 76 | fat: 2g | protein: 2g | carbs: 12g | fiber: 1g

Mama Mia Marinara Sauce

Prep time: 10 minutes | Cook time: 2 to 3 hours | Makes about 7 cups

1 medium onion, diced
2 (28-ounce / 794-g) cans no-salt-added crushed tomatoes
Ground black pepper
Salt (optional)
5 garlic cloves, minced
½ cup red wine
2 tablespoons Italian seasoning, or 1 tablespoon each dried basil and dried oregano

1. Put the onion, garlic, and tomatoes in the slow cooker. Swirl the wine in the empty tomato cans and pour everything into the slow cooker. Add the Italian seasoning, pepper, and salt (if using). Stir to combine. 2. Cover and cook on High for 2 to 3 hours or on Low for 4 to 5 hours.

Per Serving

Calories: 30 | fat: 0g | protein: 1g | carbs: 4g | fiber: 1g

Chapter 2 Breakfasts

Oatmeal Protein Mix

Prep time: 5 minutes | Cook time: 0 minutes | Serves 3

1 cup dry oatmeal
½ teaspoon cinnamon
½ teaspoon maple syrup (optional)
1 cup almond milk
2 tablespoons peanut butter (optional)
3 scoops of chocolate or vanilla flavor vegan protein powder
¼ cup almonds
2 ice cubes

1. Add the required ingredients, including the optional peanut butter if desired, to a blender. Blend for 2 minutes. Transfer to a large cup or shaker and enjoy!

Per Serving

Calories: 298 | fat: 9g | protein: 29g | carbs: 25g | fiber: 4g

Peanut Butter and Strawberry Jam Oatmeal

Prep time: 5 minutes | Cook time: 20 minutes | Serves 4

2 cups rolled oats
½ cup unsweetened plant-based milk
Pinch of salt (optional)
4 tablespoons no-sugar-added strawberry jam, divided
4 cups water
1 tablespoon maple syrup (optional)
4 tablespoons natural peanut butter, divided

1. In a medium saucepan, combine the oats and water and bring to a boil over medium-high heat. Lower the heat to medium-low and simmer, stirring often, until the oats are soft and creamy, about 15 minutes. Remove from the heat. Add the plant-based milk, maple syrup, and salt (if using) and stir well. 2. Divide the oatmeal among 4 bowls, top each with 1 tablespoon of peanut butter and 1 tablespoon of jam, and serve immediately. 3. The oatmeal can be stored in an airtight container in the refrigerator for up to 4 days. To serve, reheat the oatmeal in a medium saucepan over low heat with 2 tablespoons water to loosen it up, as oatmeal can get quite solid when chilled. Add the peanut butter and jam just before serving.

Per Serving

Calories: 284 | fat: 12g | protein: 11g | carbs: 35g| fiber: 6g

Vanilla Breakfast Smoothie

Prep time: 10 minutes | Cook time: 0 minutes | Serves 1

1 frozen banana, sliced
¼ cup old-fashioned oats
1 tablespoon flaxseed meal
3 tablespoons vanilla protein powder
1 cup vanilla almond milk
¼ cup raisins
¼ teaspoon cinnamon

1. Add all the ingredients to a blender and blend until very smooth.

Per Serving

Calories: 399 | fat: 12g | protein: 26g | carbs: 48g | fiber: 12g

Warm Maple Protein Oatmeal

Prep time: 5 minutes | Cook time: 30 minutes | Serves 2

1 cup steel-cut oats
3 tablespoons maple syrup (optional)
1 tablespoon slivered almonds
3 tablespoons raw shelled hempseed, divided
2 teaspoons cinnamon
1 tablespoon currants

1. Bring 4 cups of water to a boil in a large saucepan. Add the steel-cut oatmeal, 2 tablespoons hempseed, maple syrup (if desired), and cinnamon and bring back to a boil. Reduce heat to low and cook uncovered for 30 minutes, stirring occasionally. 2. Serve in bowls, garnished with almond slivers, currants, and the remaining hempseed.

Per Serving

Calories: 229 | fat: 6g | protein: 23g | carbs: 47g | fiber: 9g

Mango Choco Protein Pudding

Prep time: 5 minutes | Cook time: 0 minutes | Serves 2

2 cups fresh or frozen mango cubes
2 scoops soy protein isolate, chocolate flavor
3 cups water
1 peeled banana
¼ cup flaxseeds

Optional Toppings:

Blueberries
Kiwi slices
Cocoa powder

1. Add all the ingredients to a blender and blend until smooth. 2. Alternatively, blend the banana, soy isolate, 2 tablespoons of flaxseeds and the water first and divide half of the mixture between two glasses, bowls or Mason jars. 3. Scoop out the remaining banana mix into a glass or bowl and set it aside for now. 4. Blend the mango with the remaining flaxseeds. 5. Divide the mango purée between the two glasses, bowls or Mason jars, and top with the remaining banana mix. 6. Serve with the optional toppings and enjoy! 7. Store the pudding in an airtight container in the fridge, and consume within 2 days. Alternatively, store in the freezer for a maximum of 60 days and thaw at room temperature.

Per Serving

Calories: 343 | fat: 7g | protein: 31g | carbs: 39g | fiber: 8g

Savory Rosemary–Black Pepper Scones

Prep time: 10 minutes | Cook time: 20 minutes | Makes 8 scones

1 cup whole wheat flour
2 tablespoons minced fresh rosemary
½ teaspoon freshly ground black pepper
3 tablespoons puréed white beans or tahini
1 tablespoon fresh lemon juice
¾ cup old-fashioned rolled oats
½ teaspoon baking powder
½ teaspoon salt (optional)
¾ cup almond milk

1. Preheat the oven to 475°F (245°C). Lightly grease a baking sheet or use parchment paper. 2. Mix the flour, oats, rosemary, baking powder, pepper, and salt (if desired) in a medium bowl. Add the puréed white beans and use a pastry cutter, two forks, or your fingers to mix until well combined. Add the almond milk and lemon juice and mix with a fork until it forms a shaggy ball of dough; do not overmix. 3. Split the dough into two balls. Spread one ball of dough into a circle on one end of the sheet. It should be 1 inch thick. Repeat on the other side. Use a knife to cut each circle into 4 wedges. 4. Bake for 20 minutes, or until a toothpick inserted in the middle comes out clean and the scones are golden brown. Serve warm. (Toast any leftovers before serving.)

Per Serving (2 scones)

Calories: 237 | fat: 9g | protein: 10g | carbs: 41g | fiber: 7g

Almond and Protein Shake

Prep time: 5 minutes | Cook time: 0 minutes | Serves 2

1½ cups soy milk
1 teaspoon maple syrup (optional)
2 scoops of chocolate or vanilla flavor vegan protein powder
3 tablespoons almonds
1 tablespoon coconut oil (optional)
2 to 4 ice cubes
1 teaspoon cocoa powder (optional)

1. Add all the required ingredients, and if desired, the optional cocoa powder, to a blender. Blend for 2 minutes. Transfer the shake to a large cup or shaker. Serve and enjoy!

Per Serving

Calories: 340 | fat: 17g | protein: 32g | carbs: 15g | fiber: 2g

Sunrise Smoothie Bowl

Prep time: 10 minutes | Cook time: 0 minutes | Serves 2

2 cups fresh spinach
1 orange, peeled and segmented
1 ripe banana, frozen
½ cup sliced strawberries
1 kiwifruit, diced
4 fresh mint leaves, chopped
½ cup water
2 cups sliced peaches, preferably frozen
1 tablespoon fresh lemon juice
½ cup diced peaches
¼ cup raw cashews

1. In a blender, purée the spinach, water, and orange until smooth. Add the sliced peaches and the banana and pulse a few times, then purée until the mixture is thick and smooth. You will need to stop the blender occasionally to scrape down the sides. Add a little extra water if needed. The texture should be thick and creamy like frozen yogurt. 2. Divide between 2 bowls and top each with half of the strawberries, diced peaches, kiwi, cashews, and mint. Serve immediately.

Per Serving

Calories: 307 | fat: 9g | protein: 7g | carbs: 56g | fiber: 9g

Irish Breakfast Oats

Prep time: 5 minutes | Cook time: 40 minutes | Serves 4

4 cups water
1 cup gluten-free steel-cut oats
1 tablespoon almond butter
¼ teaspoon sea salt (optional)
1 tablespoon pure maple syrup (optional)

Suggested Toppings:

1 ripe banana, sliced
Dash of ground cinnamon
½ cup sliced almonds

1. In a 4-quart saucepan, bring the water and salt (if using) to a boil. Add the oats and stir well. Reduce the heat to low and cook for 30 to 40 minutes, or until cooked through. The oats will be chewy, but they should not have any crunch. 2. Stir in the maple syrup (if using) and almond butter, then spoon the oatmeal into 4 bowls. If using any suggested toppings, add them now.

Per Serving

Calories: 188 | fat: 9g | protein: 7g | carbs: 28g | fiber: 6g

Spiced Pumpkin Muffins

Prep time: 15 minutes | Cook time: 20 minutes | Makes 12 muffins

2 tablespoons ground flaxseed
1¾ cups whole wheat flour
1½ teaspoons ground cinnamon
½ teaspoon ground ginger
⅛ teaspoon ground cloves
½ cup pure maple syrup (optional)
¼ cup unsweetened nondairy milk
¼ cup water
2 teaspoons baking powder
½ teaspoon baking soda
¼ teaspoon ground nutmeg
1 cup pumpkin purée
¼ cup unsweetened applesauce
1½ teaspoons vanilla extract

1. Preheat the oven to 350°F (180°C). Line a 12-cup metal muffin pan with parchment-paper liners or use a silicone muffin pan. 2. In a small bowl, whisk together the flaxseed and water. Set aside. 3. In a large bowl, whisk together the flour, baking powder, cinnamon, baking soda, ginger, nutmeg, and cloves to combine. 4. In a medium bowl, stir together the pumpkin purée, maple syrup (if using), applesauce, milk, and vanilla. Using a spatula, fold the wet ingredients into the dry ingredients. 5. Fold the soaked flaxseed into the batter until evenly combined, but do not overmix the batter or your muffins will become dense. Spoon about ¼ cup of batter per muffin into your prepared muffin pan. 6. Bake for 18 to 20 minutes, or until a toothpick inserted into the center of a muffin comes out clean. Remove the muffins from the pan and transfer to a wire rack to cool. 7. Store in an airtight container at room temperature for up to 1 week or freeze for up to 3 months.

Per Serving (1 muffin)

Calories: 115 | fat: 1g | protein: 3g | carbs: 25g | fiber: 3g

Chocolate and Peanut Butter Quinoa

Prep time: 5 minutes | Cook time: 10 minutes | Serves 2

1 cup plant-based milk
1 tablespoon maple syrup (optional)
1 tablespoon defatted peanut powder
2 cups cooked quinoa
1 tablespoon cocoa powder

1. In a medium saucepan over medium-high heat, bring the milk to a boil. 2. Once a rolling boil is reached, reduce the heat to low, and stir in the quinoa, maple syrup (if desired), cocoa powder, and peanut powder. 3. Cook, uncovered, for 5 minutes, stirring every other minute. Serve warm.

Per Serving

Calories: 339 | fat: 8g | protein: 14g | carbs: 53g | fiber: 7g

Avocado-Chia Protein Shake

Prep time: 10 minutes | Cook time: 0 minutes | Serves 2

¼ cup dry chia seeds, soaked for at least 1 hour
½ avocado, pitted and peeled
2 scoops of chocolate flavor vegan protein powder
3 ice cubes (optional)
1 cup coconut milk
1½ tablespoon peanut butter
1 cup water
1 to 2 teaspoons cacao powder (optional)

1. Add all the required, and if desired, optional ingredients to a blender. When using ice cubes, the water can be left out. Blend for 2 minutes. Transfer the shake to a large cup or shaker. Top with some additional cacao powder. Serve and enjoy!

Per Serving

Calories: 379 | fat: 21g | protein: 30g | carbs: 17g | fiber: 10g

Pumpkin Pie Oatmeal

Prep time: 5 minutes | Cook time: 35 minutes | Serves 4

3 cups plant-based milk
1 cup unsweetened pumpkin purée
1 teaspoon ground cinnamon
⅛ teaspoon ground nutmeg
1 cup steel-cut oats
2 tablespoons maple syrup (optional)
⅛ teaspoon ground cloves

1. In a medium saucepan over medium-high heat, bring the milk to a boil. When a rolling boil is reached, reduce the heat to low, and stir in the oats, pumpkin purée, maple syrup (if desired), cinnamon, cloves, and nutmeg. 2. Cover and cook for 30 minutes, stirring every few minutes to ensure none of the oatmeal sticks to the bottom of the pot, and serve.

Per Serving

Calories: 218 | fat: 5g | protein: 7g | carbs: 38g | fiber: 6g

Muesli and Berries Bowl

Prep time: 10 minutes | Cook time: 0 minutes | Makes about 5 cups

Muesli:

1 cup rolled oats
2 cups puffed cereal
¼ cup sunflower seeds
¼ cup raisins
¼ cup chopped dried figs
¼ cup nondairy chocolate chips
1 cup spelt flakes, quinoa flakes, or more rolled oats
¼ cup almonds
¼ cup dried cranberries
¼ cup unsweetened shredded coconut
1 to 3 teaspoons ground cinnamon

Bowl:

½ cup nondairy milk or unsweetened applesauce
½ cup berries
¾ cup muesli

1. Put the muesli ingredients in a container or bag and shake. 2. Combine the muesli and bowl ingredients in a bowl or to-go container.

Per Serving (1 bowl)

Calories: 450 | fat: 11g | protein: 17g | carbs: 83g | fiber: 13g

Homemade Granola Clusters

Prep time: 15 minutes | Cook time: 1 minute | Makes 2 cups

1½ creamy or chunky cups peanut butter
1½ cups old-fashioned rolled oats
½ cup raisins
¼ cup agave or maple syrup (optional)
¾ cup flaxseed meal
¾ cup raw sunflower seeds

Optional Toppings:

¼ cup coconut shreds
Pinch of salt (optional)
1 teaspoon cinnamon

1. Add the peanut butter and maple syrup (if desired) to a medium, microwave-safe bowl. Microwave on high for 30-second intervals, stirring between intervals until the mixture is creamy and well combined. 2. Add the oats, flaxseed meal, raisins, and sunflower seeds, and stir together with a spoon until thoroughly combined. 3. Transfer the mixture to a baking sheet. 4. Place in the freezer for at least 25 minutes. Store in the refrigerator in an airtight container for up to 7 days.

Per Serving (¼ cup)

Calories: 510 | fat: 29g | protein: 31g | carbs: 34g | fiber: 11g

Sweet Potato Pie Oatmeal

Prep time: 10 minutes | Cook time: 22 minutes | Serves 2

1 large sweet potato, peeled and diced
1 cup unsweetened almond milk
½ teaspoon ground cinnamon
¼ teaspoon orange zest
Pinch salt (optional)
1 cup rolled oats
½ cup date molasses
½ teaspoon ground ginger
¼ teaspoon ground allspice

1. Steam or boil the sweet potato until tender, about 10 minutes. Drain and mash it and add it to a small saucepan with the oats, almond milk, molasses, cinnamon, ginger, orange zest, allspice, and salt (if using). Cook the mixture over medium heat until the oats are tender, 10 to 12 minutes.

Per Serving
Calories: 400 | fat: 3g | protein: 13g | carbs: 84g | fiber: 9g

Strawberry, Banana, and Granola Yogurt Bowls

Prep time: 10 minutes | Cook time: 0 minutes | Serves 2

2 cups plain plant-based yogurt
2 tablespoons maple syrup (optional)
1 medium banana, sliced
1 cup granola
1 cup sliced strawberries

1. Divide the yogurt between 2 serving bowls. Top each bowl with ½ cup of granola and drizzle with 1 tablespoon of maple syrup (if using). Divide the strawberries and bananas between the bowls and serve immediately.

Per Serving
Calories: 391 | fat: 8g | protein: 12g | carbs: 66g | fiber: 9g

To the Power of Four Overnight Oats

Prep time: 10 minutes | Cook time: 0 minutes | Serves 2

3½ cups unsweetened almond milk
¼ cup maple syrup (optional)
2 tablespoons unsweetened shredded coconut
4 tablespoons peanut butter, divided
2 cups old-fashioned oats
2 tablespoons chia seeds
¼ cup sunflower seed kernels
Sunflower seed kernels, for garnish (optional)

1. Add all the ingredients except for 2 tablespoons of the peanut butter and the sunflower seeds to a large bowl. Mix well. It will seem very wet but the chia seeds and oats will absorb some of the milk. Cover and place in the refrigerator to set overnight. 2. To serve in the morning, dot the remaining 2 tablespoons peanut butter around the inside of two bowls and fill each with the overnight oats. Garnish with sunflower seeds, if desired.

Per Serving
Calories: 559 | fat: 21g | protein: 24g | carbs: 46g | fiber: 10g

Chocolate Quinoa Breakfast Bowl

Prep time: 5 minutes | Cook time: 25 to 30 minutes | Serves 2

1 cup quinoa
1 cup nondairy milk
1 large banana
1 to 2 tablespoons almond butter, or other nut or seed butter
¼ cup raspberries
1 teaspoon ground cinnamon
1 cup water
2 to 3 tablespoons unsweetened cocoa powder
1 tablespoon ground flaxseed, or chia or hemp seeds
2 tablespoons walnuts

1. Put the quinoa, cinnamon, milk, and water in a medium pot. Bring to a boil over high heat, then turn down low and simmer, covered, for 25 to 30 minutes. 2. While the quinoa is simmering, purée or mash the banana in a medium bowl and stir in the cocoa powder, almond butter, and flaxseed. 3. To serve, spoon 1 cup cooked quinoa into a bowl, top with half the pudding and half the walnuts and raspberries.

Per Serving

Calories: 564 | fat: 17g | protein: 21g | carbs: 86g | fiber: 13g

Baked Flaxseed-Battered French Toast

Prep time: 10 minutes | Cook time: 15 minutes | Serves 4

¼ cup ground flaxseeds
Olive oil cooking spray
1 teaspoon vanilla extract
8 slices whole-grain bread
1½ cups unsweetened plant-based milk, divided
1 tablespoon ground cinnamon
3 tablespoons maple syrup, plus more for serving (optional)

1. In a medium bowl, combine the flaxseeds and ½ cup of plant-based milk. Let the mixture stand for 10 minutes to give the flaxseeds time to absorb the liquid and thicken, which will give them an consistency. 2. Preheat the oven to 400°F (205°C). Spray a sheet pan with olive oil cooking spray. 3. Add the remaining 1 cup plant-based milk, the cinnamon, vanilla, and maple syrup (if using) to the flax mixture and mix until combined. Dip each slice of bread into the flax mixture, making sure to completely cover in the liquid. Let any excess drip back into the bowl and then put the slices on the sheet pan. 4. Bake for 10 minutes. Using a spatula, carefully flip the bread and bake for 5 minutes. Serve with maple syrup.

Per Serving

Calories: 272 | fat: 7g | protein: 11g | carbs: 42g | fiber: 7g

Chapter 3 Vegetables and Sides

Portabella Mushroom Gyro

Prep time: 15 minutes | Cook time: 15 minutes | Serves 2

Vegetables:
2 large portabella mushroom caps
1 teaspoon ground cumin
½ teaspoon dried oregano
¼ cup diced red onion
2 tablespoons vegan Worcestershire sauce
1 teaspoon maple syrup (optional)
1 tablespoon coconut oil (optional)
½ red bell pepper, diced large

Fresh White Sauce:
½ cup vegan mayonnaise
1 tablespoon lemon juice
¼ teaspoon dill weed
¼ cup raw shelled hempseeds
¼ teaspoon dried mint

Assemble:
2 pita flatbreads
1 ounce (28 g) baby spinach

Make Vegetables: 1. Remove the stems from the mushrooms and also remove the gills with a spoon. Discard. Slice the mushrooms into thick strips. 2. Mix the Worcestershire sauce, cumin, maple syrup (if desired), and oregano in a medium bowl. Lay the mushroom slices in the marinade and let marinate for 10 minutes. 3. Heat the oil (if desired) in a large skillet over medium-high heat. Add the onion and bell pepper and sauté for 10 minutes. Add the marinated mushroom slices and sauté for 5 more minutes. Remove from the heat and let cool. Make Fresh White Sauce: 4. Mix all of the Fresh White Sauce ingredients in a small bowl and set aside. Assemble: 5. Lay out a layer of spinach leaves on each flatbread. Spoon the Fresh White Sauce down the center. Lay the mushroom and bell pepper mixture on top. Fold each flatbread to overlap and secure with decorative picks.

Per Serving

Calories: 374 | fat: 26g | protein: 16g | carbs: 27g | fiber: 4g

Spiced Green Peas and Yams

Prep time: 15 minutes | Cook time: 20 minutes | Serves 4

3 medium white yams, cut into ½-inch dice (about 2 cups)
1 pinch asafetida (optional)
¼ teaspoon garam masala
½ teaspoon ground cumin
½ tablespoon fresh lime juice
½ cup green peas
¾ teaspoon cumin seeds, toasted
¼ teaspoon cayenne pepper
½ teaspoon ground coriander
½ teaspoon salt, or to taste (optional)
½ tablespoon finely chopped cilantro

1. Steam the yams in a double boiler or steamer basket for 5 to 7 minutes, or until tender. Set aside. 2. In a small saucepan, bring 1 cup of water to a boil, add the peas, and cook for 5 to 10 minutes, until the peas are soft. Drain and set aside. 3. In a large skillet over medium heat, place the cumin seeds, asafetida, white yams, peas, cayenne pepper, garam masala, coriander, cumin, and salt (if using). Add 2 tablespoons of water, mix well, and cook for another 2 to 3 minutes, or until the water has evaporated. Stir in the lime juice and mix well. Serve garnished with the cilantro.

Per Serving

Calories: 107 | fat: 0g | protein: 2g | carbs: 24g | fiber: 4g

Spicy Butternut Squash Bisque

Prep time: 10 minutes | Cook time: 30 minutes | Serves 4

Olive oil cooking spray
2 garlic cloves, peeled
1 teaspoon smoked paprika
4 cups unsweetened plant-based milk
2 tablespoons tomato paste
4 tablespoons chopped cilantro leaves, for garnish
4 tablespoons pepitas, for garnish (optional)
1 large butternut squash, peeled, seeded and cut into 1-inch cubes (about 3 cups)
½ teaspoon salt (optional)
2 tablespoons nutritional yeast
1 teaspoon sriracha
4 tablespoons plain plant-based yogurt, for garnish

1. Preheat the oven to 400°F (205°C). Spray a sheet pan with olive oil cooking spray. 2. Combine the squash, garlic, smoked paprika, and salt (if using) on the sheet pan and toss until evenly coated. Bake for 10 minutes. Using a spatula, turn the squash and continue to bake for another 10 minutes, or until cooked through. 3. Transfer the squash and garlic to a blender. Add the plant-based milk, nutritional yeast, tomato paste, and sriracha and purée until smooth and creamy. Pour the mixture into a large saucepan and cook over medium heat until warm. Taste and adjust the seasonings, if desired. 4. Portion the soup into 4 bowls, garnish each with 1 tablespoon each of cilantro, yogurt, pepitas, and serve.

Per Serving

Calories: 141 | fat: 3g | protein: 8g | carbs: 24g | fiber: 3g

Vegetable Spring Rolls with Spicy Peanut Dipping Sauce

Prep time: 15 minutes | Cook time: 10 minutes | Serves 2

Spicy Peanut Dipping Sauce:
2 tablespoons defatted peanut powder
1 tablespoon rice vinegar
½ teaspoon garlic powder
1 tablespoon maple syrup (optional)
½ teaspoon onion powder
½ teaspoon red pepper flakes

Spring Rolls:
6 rice paper wraps
1½ cups cooked brown rice
1 bunch fresh cilantro
1 bunch fresh basil
6 large lettuce leaves
1 cup shredded carrots
1 bunch fresh mint

Make Spicy Peanut Dipping Sauce: 1. In a small saucepan over medium heat, combine the peanut powder, maple syrup (if desired), rice vinegar, onion powder, garlic powder, and red pepper flakes. Cook for 10 minutes, stirring occasionally. Remove the sauce from the heat, and set aside to cool. Make Spring Rolls: 1. Fill a shallow bowl or pan with warm water, and dip a rice paper wrap in the water for 10 to 15 seconds. Remove and place on a cutting board or other clean, smooth surface. 2. Lay a lettuce leaf down flat on a rice paper wrap, then add ¼ cup of brown rice, 2 to 3 tablespoons of shredded carrots, and a few leaves each of cilantro, mint, and basil. 3. Wrap the sides of the rice paper halfway into the center, then roll the wrap from the bottom to the top to form a tight roll. 4. Repeat for the remaining spring rolls. Serve with the sauce in a dipping bowl on the side.

Per Serving

Calories: 263 | fat: 3g | protein: 11g | carbs: 46g | fiber: 5g

Mixed Winter Vegetables with Spicy Poppy Seed Sauce

Prep time: 20 minutes | Cook time: 25 minutes | Serves 4 to 6

1 cup green beans, trimmed, cut into ¼-inch pieces
1 medium potato, chopped (about 1 cup)
½ teaspoon cumin seeds
1 small yellow onion, peeled and finely chopped
½ teaspoon grated ginger
⅛ teaspoon ground cinnamon
¼ teaspoon freshly ground black pepper, or to taste
1 medium tomato, chopped (about 1 cup)
2 tablespoons raw cashews, finely ground
1 tablespoon chopped cilantro
2 carrots, peeled and sliced
1 cup cauliflower florets
3 tablespoons white poppy seeds
1 clove garlic, peeled and minced
⅛ teaspoon ground cloves
Pinch ground cardamom
½ teaspoon turmeric
1 teaspoon salt, or to taste (optional)
½ tablespoon fresh lime juice

1. Steam the green beans, carrot, potato, and cauliflower in a double boiler or steamer basket for 8 to 10 minutes, or until tender. Set aside. 2. In a dry skillet over medium-low heat, toast the cumin seeds for 2 minutes. Add the poppy seeds and toast for another 2 to 3 minutes until the poppy seeds begin to brown. Remove from the heat and let cool. Combine the toasted seeds, onion, garlic, ginger, cloves, cinnamon, cardamom, pepper, and turmeric in a blender and process into a thick paste. Add the paste to a large skillet and cook on medium heat for 5 to 7 minutes. 3. Add the tomato to the blender and purée until smooth. Add the tomato purée and salt (if using) to the onion paste in the skillet and cook for another 2 to 3 minutes. Add the cashew powder and cook for 2 minutes. Add the steamed vegetables, lime juice, and 1½ cups of water, and bring the mixture to a boil. Remove the pan from the heat, and serve garnished with the cilantro

Per Serving

Calories: 97 | fat: 3g | protein: 3g | carbs: 15g | fiber: 4g

Crispy Maple Mustard Cabbage

Prep time: 5 minutes | Cook time: 40 minutes | Serves 6

2 tablespoons virgin olive oil (optional)
1½ teaspoons pure maple syrup (optional)
Salt and pepper, to taste (optional)
1 tablespoon grainy mustard
½ head large cabbage or 1 small whole cabbage

1. Preheat the oven to 400°F (205°C). 2. In a small bowl, whisk together the olive oil, grainy mustard, and maple syrup, if using. 3. Cut the cabbage into 1-inch wedges. Once you have the wedges, remove most of the core, leaving a thin strip intact so that the wedge holds together through the roasting process. 4. Lay the wedges on a large baking sheet. Brush the side facing up with the olive oil mixture. Season with salt and pepper, if using. Slide the baking sheet into the oven, and roast for 20 minutes. 5. Remove the baking sheet from the oven, and carefully flip the wedges over with a spatula. Brush with the remaining olive oil mixture. Slide the baking sheet back into the oven, and roast for another 20 minutes or until the cabbage wedges are quite browned and have crispy edges. Serve the cabbage warm.

Per Serving

Calories: 75 | fat: 5g | protein: 2g | carbs: 8g | fiber: 2g

Baked Spaghetti Squash with Swiss Chard

Prep time: 15 minutes | Cook time: 55 minutes | Serves 4

2 small spaghetti squash (about 1 pound / 454 g each), halved
1 medium yellow onion, peeled and diced small
4 cloves garlic, peeled and minced
2 teaspoons ground coriander
½ teaspoon crushed red pepper flakes
Salt and freshly ground black pepper, to taste
1 large bunch red-ribbed Swiss chard
1 red bell pepper, seeded and diced small
2 teaspoons ground cumin
½ teaspoon paprika
Zest and juice of 1 lemon

1. Preheat the oven to 350°F (180°C). 2. Season the cut sides of the squash with salt and pepper. Place the squash halves, cut side down, on a rimmed baking sheet. Add ½ cup of water to the pan and bake the squash for 45 to 55 minutes, or until very tender (the squash is done when it can be easily pierced with a knife). 3. While the squash is baking, remove the stems from the chard and chop them. Chop the leaves into bite-size pieces and set them aside. Place the onion, red pepper, and chard stems in a large saucepan and sauté over medium heat for 5 minutes. Add water 1 to 2 tablespoons at a time to keep the vegetables from sticking to the pan. Add the garlic, cumin, coriander, paprika, and crushed red pepper flakes and cook for 3 minutes. Add the chard leaves and lemon zest and juice. Season with salt and pepper and cook until the chard is wilted, about 5 minutes. Remove from the heat. 4. When the squash is finished baking, scoop out the flesh (it should come away looking like noodles) and stir it into the warm chard mixture.

Per Serving

Calories: 36 | fat: 0g | protein: 1g | carbs: 7g | fiber: 1g

Vegan Goulash

Prep time: 20 minutes | Cook time: 50 minutes | Serves 5

5 tablespoons olive oil (optional)
1 head garlic, minced
10 small tomatoes, cubed
½ cup dry red wine
10 medium potatoes, skinned, cubed
Salt and pepper to taste (optional)
12 medium onions, finely chopped
4 red bell peppers, cored and chopped
4 tablespoons paprika powder
3 to 6 cups vegetable broth
1 (7-ounce / 198-g) pack tempeh
¼ cup fresh parsley, chopped

1. Heat the olive oil, in a large pot over medium heat. Sauté the onions until brown. Add the minced garlic and stir for 1 minute. Continue to add the chopped bell peppers and cook the ingredients for another 3 minutes while stirring. Blend in the tomatoes, paprika powder, salt (if desired), pepper and the dry red wine. Stir thoroughly while letting the mixture cook for another 2 minutes. Add the vegetable broth and the potato cubes to the pot and stir to combine all ingredients. Put a lid on the pot and allow the goulash to cook for another 5 minutes. 2. Turn the heat down to low and continue to gently cook the goulash for 15 minutes. The goulash will thicken and the potatoes will get cooked properly. Add the tempeh and taste to see if the goulash needs more salt and pepper. Let the goulash cook for another 15 minutes. Check if the potatoes have softened with a fork. Cook the mixture a few minutes more if the potatoes are hard to penetrate. Once the potatoes are soft, add the parsley, stir and take the goulash off the heat. 3. Allow the goulash to cool down for about 10 minutes and serve or allow the goulash to cool down longer before storing.

Per Serving

Calories: 591 | fat: 18g | protein: 16g | carbs: 74g | fiber: 14g

Ugly Veggie Mash

Prep time: 10 minutes | Cook time: 25 minutes | Serves 8

1 pound (454 g) parsnips, peeled, trimmed, and cut into 1-inch pieces
1 large celeriac, peeled using a paring knife and chopped into 1-inch cubes
1 large rutabaga, peeled and chopped into 1-inch cubes
2 cups vegetable broth
Salt and black pepper (optional)

1. Place the parsnips, rutabaga, and celeriac in a large pot with a tight-fitting lid. Add the broth, cover, and bring to a boil over high heat. Reduce the heat to low and cook until the vegetables are fork-tender and most of the liquid has evaporated, 20 to 25 minutes. 2. Mash with a potato masher or serving fork, season with salt and pepper, if desired and serve.

Per Serving

Calories: 82 | fat: 0g | protein: 2g | carbs: 19g | fiber: 5g

Spicy Miso-Roasted Tomatoes and Eggplant

Prep time: 25 minutes | Cook time: 50 minutes | Serves 6

1 medium eggplant, cut into 1 x 3-inch wedges
1 medium yellow onion, cut into ¼-inch slices
2 tablespoons unpasteurized sweet white miso
2 tablespoons mirin, or 1 teaspoon maple syrup (optional)
1 teaspoon ground coriander
½ teaspoon ground turmeric
¾ cup cooked chickpeas, well drained
4 medium tomatoes, cut into 6 wedges each
3 tablespoons melted extra-virgin coconut oil or olive oil (optional)
1 tablespoon freshly squeezed lemon juice
1 large garlic clove, grated or pressed
1 teaspoon red chili pepper flakes
½ teaspoon fine sea salt, plus more to taste (optional)
Chopped fresh flat-leaf parsley or cilantro leaves for garnish

1. Preheat the oven to 400°F (205°C). 2. Line a large baking sheet with parchment paper and put the eggplant, tomatoes, and onion on it. Combine the oil, miso, mirin, lemon juice, garlic, coriander, red chili pepper flakes, turmeric, and salt, if using, in a small bowl and stir until smooth. Pour over the vegetables and toss until evenly coated. Spread the vegetables out on the pan; they should almost be in a single layer, with just a few overlapping. 3. Roast for 20 to 25 minutes, until the vegetables are browned on the bottom. Remove the vegetables from the oven and turn them over as best you can; you may end up just stirring them, as they will be juicy. Roast for another 15 to 20 minutes, until the vegetables are completely soft and browned in spots. Scatter the chickpeas over the vegetables, sprinkle with a little more salt, if using, and return to the oven for 5 more minutes to warm the chickpeas through. Transfer the vegetables to a serving platter and top with the herbs. Serve warm or at room temperature. Any leftovers can be stored in an airtight container in the fridge for up to 3 days.

Per Serving

Calories: 152 | fat: 8g | protein: 4g | carbs: 18g | fiber: 6g

Ginger, Shiitake, Pecan, and Apricot Pilaf

Prep time: 15 minutes | Cook time: 3 hours | Serves 4 to 6

1 small onion, diced
2 carrots, diced
2 cups brown rice
1 teaspoon garlic powder
6 cups store-bought low-sodium vegetable broth
4 ounces (113 g) shiitake mushrooms, stemmed
1 cup chopped pecans
½ bunch flat-leaf parsley, coarsely chopped
2 celery stalks, diced
1 cup wild rice
1 (1-inch) piece fresh ginger, peeled and minced, or 1 teaspoon ground ginger
1 tablespoon low-sodium soy sauce, tamari, or coconut aminos
½ cup chopped dried apricots

1. Put the onion, celery, and carrots in the slow cooker. Add the wild rice, brown rice, ginger, garlic powder, broth, and soy sauce. 2. Slice the mushroom caps into strips and add to the slow cooker. Stir to combine. Cover and cook on High for 3 hours or on Low for 5 to 6 hours, until all of the liquid is absorbed. Fluff with a fork and top with the pecans, apricots, and parsley to serve.

Per Serving

Calories: 757 | fat: 24g | protein: 19g | carbs: 126g | fiber: 15g

Savory Slow Cooker Stuffing

Prep time: 20 minutes | Cook time: 4 hours 45 minutes | Serves 5 to 7

Nonstick cooking spray (optional)
2 tablespoons ground flaxseed
5 tablespoons water
6 large celery stalks, diced (about 2 cups)
2 teaspoons dried sage
1 teaspoon poultry seasoning
1 teaspoon crushed or ground fennel seed
Ground black pepper
3½ to 5 cups store-bought low-sodium vegetable broth, divided
2 (12-ounce / 340-g) packages stuffing cubes (about 12 cups)
2 small or 1 large onion, diced (about 2 cups)
1 (8-ounce / 227-g) package white button mushrooms, diced
1 teaspoon marjoram
⅓ cup chopped fresh parsley
Salt (optional)

1. Coat the inside of the slow cooker with cooking spray (if using) or line it with a slow cooker liner. Place the dry stuffing cubes in the slow cooker. In a small bowl, stir together the flaxseed and water to make 2 flax eggs. Set aside. 2. In a cast-iron or nonstick skillet over medium-high heat, dry sauté the onions, celery, and mushrooms for 5 to 7 minutes, or until the onions are translucent, adding a splash of water or broth to avoid sticking. Stir in the sage, poultry seasoning, marjoram, fennel seed, parsley, pepper, and salt (if using) and cook for another minute or so. Transfer the mixture to the slow cooker and add 3½ cups of broth, stirring to combine. Add more broth, ½ cup at a time, to achieve your desired consistency. 3. Cover and cook on High for 45 minutes, then turn the heat to Low and cook for 3 to 4 hours, until the stuffing reaches the consistency you prefer. Add more broth as needed during the cooking time for a moister stuffing.

Per Serving

Calories: 523 | fat: 7g | protein: 20g | carbs: 77g | fiber: 10g

Cumin-Citrus Roasted Carrots

Prep time: 10 minutes | Cook time: 30 minutes | Serves 6

8 large carrots, sliced into ½-inch rounds
¼ cup vegetable broth
¼ teaspoon ground turmeric
1 tablespoon fresh lime juice
¼ cup orange juice
1 teaspoon ground cumin
Salt and black pepper (optional)
Chopped flat-leaf parsley (optional)

1. Preheat the oven to 400°F (205°C). 2. Place the carrots in a large baking dish, then add the orange juice, broth, cumin, and turmeric. Season with salt and pepper, if desired. 3. Bake, uncovered, until the carrots are lightly browned and the juices have reduced slightly, about 30 minutes, stirring halfway through. Drizzle with the lime juice and parsley, if desired, and serve.

Per Serving

Calories: 47 | fat: 0g | protein: 1g | carbs: 11g | fiber: 3g

Loaded Frijoles

Prep time: 10 minutes | Cook time: 20 minutes | Serves 6

1 tablespoon avocado oil (optional)
3 garlic cloves, minced
1 teaspoon ground cumin
¼ cup tomato sauce
1 yellow onion, finely chopped
2 teaspoons chili powder
2 (15-ounce / 425-g) cans pinto beans, undrained
Sea salt, to taste (optional)

1. In a 4-quart pan, warm the avocado oil (if using) over medium-high heat. Add the onion and sauté for 5 minutes. 2. Add the garlic and cook for 30 seconds, then add the chili powder and cumin and cook for 30 seconds. 3. Stir in the beans and tomato sauce. Taste and add salt (if using), if needed. 4. Mash the beans, or purée them with an immersion blender, until the desired consistency is reached. Cook over medium-low heat for 15 minutes, or until the beans thicken. If the beans become too thick, add a little water. 5. Store in an airtight container in the fridge for up to 1 week or in the freezer for several months.

Per Serving

Calories: 142 | fat: 3g | protein: 7g | carbs: 22g | fiber: 6g

Grilled Eggplant "Steaks"

Prep time: 10 minutes | Cook time: 10 minutes | Serves 4

3 tablespoons balsamic vinegar
2 tablespoons low-sodium soy sauce
1 large eggplant, stemmed and cut into ¾-inch slices
Juice of 1 lemon
Freshly ground black pepper, to taste

1. Prepare the grill. 2. Combine the balsamic vinegar, lemon juice, soy sauce, and pepper in a small bowl. 3. Brush both sides of the eggplant slices with the marinade. 4. Place the eggplant on the hot grill and cook on each side for 4 to 5 minutes, brushing periodically with additional marinade.

Per Serving

Calories: 51 | fat: 0g | protein: 2g | carbs: 11g | fiber: 4g

Chapter 4 Vegetarian Mains

Stacked Enchilada Casserole

Prep time: 30 minutes | Cook time: 1 hour | Serves 4

Filling:

1 cup diced yellow bell pepper
1 cup diced white onion
1 tablespoon extra virgin olive oil (optional)
¼ teaspoon ground black pepper
2 ounces (57 g) tempeh, pulsed fine
1 teaspoon ground cumin
2 cloves garlic, minced
6 small corn tortillas
1 sweet potato, peeled and chopped into bite-size pieces
1 teaspoon salt, divided (optional)
1 1(15 ounces / 425 g) can black beans, drained and rinsed
1 teaspoon chili powder
2 cups store-bought red enchilada sauce

White Sauce:

2 tablespoons dairy-free butter
1½ cups dairy-free milk
3 tablespoons flour
1 tablespoon nutritional yeast

Make Filling: 1. Preheat the oven to 400°F (205°C). 2. Place the bell pepper, sweet potato, and onion on a baking sheet. Sprinkle with the oil (if desired) and toss to make sure all the vegetables are coated. Spread out on the baking sheet and season with ½ teaspoon salt (if desired) and pepper. Place in the oven and roast for 15 minutes. Remove from the oven, stir, and return to the oven for another 15 minutes. Check to see if sweet potatoes can be easily pierced with a fork. If not, stir and cook for up to another 10 minutes. Remove from the oven and set aside. Lower the oven temperature to 350°F (180°C). 3. Add the roasted vegetables, beans, tempeh, cumin, chili powder, and garlic to a medium bowl. 4. Spread ¼ cup enchilada sauce in the bottom of an 8-inch square glass casserole dish. 5. Cut four tortillas into fourths. Lay four of the quarters in each corner of the casserole with the V toward the corner. Lay one whole tortilla right in the center. Top with a third of the vegetable mixture and spread evenly over the tortillas. Drizzle another ¼ cup of the enchilada sauce. Lay another layer of tortillas as you did before. Top with another layer using a third of the vegetable mixture and drizzle on another ¼ cup enchilada sauce. Lay another layer of tortillas and then the remainder of the vegetable mixture. Keep the remaining enchilada sauce aside. Make White Sauce: 6. Melt the butter in a medium saucepan. Stir in the flour and cook for 1 minute. Add the milk and heat over medium-high heat to a low boil. Add the nutritional yeast and continue to cook and stir until the sauce thickens and cooks down by about ¼ cup. Remove from the heat. Assemble: 7. Pour the remaining enchilada sauce over the top of the casserole and spread evenly. Drizzle the white sauce back and forth over the top but do not spread. Cover with either the lid to the casserole dish or a sheet of aluminum foil. Bake for 30 minutes. 8. Take the enchilada casserole out of the oven and also remove the foil. Let sit for 10 minutes before serving in squares.

Per Serving

Calories: 439 | fat: 18g | protein: 20g | carbs: 45g | fiber: 10g

Rainbow Shepherd's Pie

Prep time: 15 minutes | Cook time: 45 minutes | Serves 4

Topping:

4 medium sweet potatoes, peeled and diced (about 4 cups)
2 tablespoons nutritional yeast
½ teaspoon salt (optional)
1 teaspoon garlic powder
¼ cup unsweetened plant-based milk

Filling:

1 (8-ounce / 227-g) package tempeh
½ small yellow onion, diced small
1 large carrot, peeled and diced small
½ cup frozen peas
2 tablespoons tomato paste
2 cups water
2 teaspoons extra-virgin olive oil (optional)
½ red or yellow bell pepper, diced small
½ cup frozen corn
2 tablespoons whole-wheat flour
2 tablespoons low-sodium soy sauce or gluten-free tamari

1. Preheat the oven to 375°F (190°C). 2. Make the Topping: Put the sweet potatoes in a medium saucepan and cover with enough water to cover completely. Bring to a boil over high heat. Lower the heat to medium and cook until the sweet potatoes are tender, about 15 minutes. Drain and return the potatoes to the saucepan. Add the salt (if using), garlic powder, nutritional yeast, and plant-based milk and, using a potato masher, mash until creamy. Set aside. 3. Make the Filling: While the potatoes are cooking, in a blender or food processor, pulse the tempeh into very small pieces. 4. In a large skillet over medium heat, heat the oil. Add the tempeh and onion and cook, stirring often, until the onion and tempeh are lightly browned, about 10 minutes. Add the bell pepper, carrot, corn, and peas and cook until the peppers are fragrant, about 5 minutes. 5. Add the flour and stir until well combined. Add the tomato paste, soy sauce, and water and bring to a boil. Lower the heat to medium and cook, stirring often, until a thick gravy forms. 6. Assemble the Dish: In an 8-by-8-inch baking dish, spread out the tempeh and veggie mixture. Top with the mashed sweet potatoes, spreading it to the edges. Cover with aluminum foil and bake for 15 minutes, until bubbly.

Per Serving

Calories: 322 | fat: 9g | protein: 17g | carbs: 48g | fiber: 7g

Mango-Ginger Chickpea Curry

Prep time: 5 minutes | Cook time: 15 minutes | Serves 6

3 cups cooked chickpeas
2 cups plant-based milk
1 tablespoon curry powder
1 teaspoon ground coriander
1 teaspoon onion powder
2 cups mango chunks
2 tablespoons maple syrup (optional)
1 tablespoon ground ginger
1 teaspoon garlic powder
⅛ teaspoon ground cinnamon

1. Heat a large stockpot or Dutch oven over medium heat. 2. In the pot, combine the chickpeas, mango, milk, maple syrup (if desired), curry powder, ginger, coriander, garlic powder, onion powder, and cinnamon. Cover and cook for 10 minutes, stirring after about 5 minutes. 3. Uncover and cook for an additional 5 minutes, stirring every other minute. Serve.

Per Serving

Calories: 219 | fat: 4g | protein: 8g | carbs: 38g | fiber: 9g

Chickpea and Cauliflower Fajitas

Prep time: 10 minutes | Cook time: 30 minutes | Serves 4

1 tablespoon extra-virgin olive oil (optional)
1 small yellow onion, thinly sliced
1 red bell pepper, seeded and thinly sliced
1 teaspoon chili powder
½ teaspoon garlic powder
12 (6-inch) soft corn tortillas, for serving
½ bunch cilantro, chopped, for serving
½ large head cauliflower, cut into small florets (about 2 cups)
1 (15-ounce / 425-g) can chickpeas, drained and rinsed
½ teaspoon smoked paprika
1 teaspoon salt (optional)
1 avocado, pitted, peeled, quartered, and thinly sliced, for serving

1. In a large sauté pan, heat the oil over medium heat. Add the cauliflower and cook until it begins to brown, about 5 minutes. Add the onion and cook, stirring occasionally, for 5 minutes. Add the bell pepper and cook, stirring occasionally, until the cauliflower is fork-tender, about 5 minutes. 2. Add the chickpeas, chili powder, smoked paprika, garlic powder, and salt (if using) and stir until combined. Cook until the spices flavor the mixture, about 5 minutes. Transfer the fajita mixture to a serving bowl. 3. Wipe out the sauté pan with a paper towel and warm the tortillas over medium heat until they are pliable, about 2 minutes per side. 4. Divide the filling among the tortillas, top each one with 2 or 3 slices of avocado and some chopped cilantro, and serve.

Per Serving

Calories: 500 | fat: 18g | protein: 15g | carbs: 73g | fiber: 13g

The Best Veggie Burgers

Prep time: 15 minutes | Cook time: 30 minutes | Makes 12 patties

1 yellow onion, coarsely chopped
1 sweet potato, skin on, cubed
1 cup precooked brown rice
1 tablespoon paprika
2 tablespoons tomato paste
1 tablespoon Dijon mustard or yellow mustard
¾ to 1 cup coarse cornmeal
3 garlic cloves, coarsely chopped
½ cup walnuts
2 cups precooked green lentils or brown lentils
1 tablespoon tamari
¼ cup water
¼ cup ground flaxseed

1. Preheat the oven to 450°F (235°C). Line a baking sheet with parchment paper. 2. In a food processor, combine the onion, garlic, sweet potato, and walnuts. Process for 1 to 2 minutes, or until the ingredients are combined and have the consistency of rice. 3. Add the brown rice, cooked lentils, paprika, and tamari. Pulse several times to incorporate the ingredients. 4. In a large bowl, stir together the tomato paste, water, mustard, and flaxseed. Add the blended ingredients to the bowl and mix to combine fully. 5. Starting with ¾ cup, stir in the cornmeal, adding more if the mixture looks too wet. The dough should form a ball without sticking to your hands too much. Divide the dough into 12 equal portions, roughly ¼ cup each. Roll the portions into balls and flatten onto the prepared baking sheet. 6. Bake for 15 minutes. Flip the patties and bake for 15 minutes more. The patties should be browned on the outside and firm to the touch. Serve immediately or let cool completely before freezing in an airtight container for up to 3 months.

Per Serving (1 burger)

Calories: 161 | fat: 5g | protein: 6g | carbs: 24g | fiber: 6g

Baked Taquitos with Fat-Free Refried Beans

Prep time: 5 minutes | Cook time: 25 minutes | Serves 4

2 cups cooked pinto beans
1 teaspoon ground cumin
½ teaspoon onion powder
12 corn tortillas
1 teaspoon chili powder
½ teaspoon garlic powder
¼ teaspoon red pepper flakes

1. Preheat the oven to 400°F (205°C). Line a baking sheet with parchment paper. 2. Combine the beans, chili powder, cumin, garlic powder, onion powder, and red pepper flakes in a food processor or blender. Pulse or blend on low for 30 seconds, or until smooth, then set aside. 3. Place the tortillas on the baking sheet, and bake for 1 to 2 minutes. This helps soften the tortillas and makes rolling them much easier. 4. Remove the tortillas from the oven, then add a couple of heaping tablespoons of the refried beans to the bottom half of each corn tortilla. Roll the tortillas tightly, and place them back on the baking sheet, seam-side down. 5. Bake for 20 minutes, turning once after about 10 minutes, and serve.

Per Serving

Calories: 286 | fat: 3g | protein: 12g | carbs: 56g | fiber: 13g

Chickpea, Butternut Squash, and Herb Stuffed Peppers

Prep time: 5 minutes | Cook time: 40 minutes | Serves 4

2 teaspoons extra-virgin olive oil (optional)
3 garlic cloves, minced
2 cups frozen cubed butternut squash
1 teaspoon maple syrup (optional)
1 teaspoon salt (optional)
2 tablespoons chopped fresh parsley
2 cups finely chopped baby spinach
1 cup frozen or cooked brown rice
½ small yellow onion, diced small
1 (15-ounce / 425-g) can chickpeas, drained and rinsed
1 teaspoon smoked paprika
¼ cup plus 2 tablespoons water, divided
1 teaspoon Italian seasoning
2 tablespoons chopped fresh mint
Juice of 1 lemon
4 large red or yellow bell peppers

1. In a large skillet, heat the olive oil over medium heat. Add the onion and garlic and cook, stirring often, until fragrant, about 5 minutes. Add the chickpeas, squash, smoked paprika, maple syrup (if using), and ¼ cup of water and cook, stirring constantly, for 5 minutes. 2. Remove from the heat and add the salt (if using), Italian seasoning, parsley, mint, spinach, and lemon juice. Add the brown rice and mix well. 3. Preheat the oven to 400°F (205°C). 4. Rinse the bell peppers and pat dry with paper towels. Cut about 2 inches off the top of each pepper. Remove and discard the seeds. Spoon equal amounts of the vegetable-rice mixture into the peppers, packing it in tightly. Cover with the pepper tops. 5. Transfer the stuffed peppers into an 8-by-8-inch baking dish. Pour the remaining 2 tablespoons water into the bottom of the baking dish. Cover the dish with aluminum foil and bake for 30 minutes. Serve hot.

Per Serving

Calories: 254 | fat: 5g | protein: 9g | carbs: 49g | fiber: 8g

Black Bean Patties with Carrots and Corn

Prep time: 15 minutes | Cook time: 15 minutes | Serves 6

1½ cups fresh bread crumbs
2 tablespoons coconut oil, divided (optional)
½ cup finely diced carrot
½ teaspoon dried oregano
¼ teaspoon ground cumin
2 cloves garlic, finely diced
¼ cup sunflower seed kernels
2 tablespoons raw shelled hempseed
Condiments and toppings of your choice
2 tablespoons chia seeds
1 cup diced yellow onion
1 ear of corn, kernels cut from the cob
2 teaspoons chili powder
1 teaspoon salt (optional)
1 (28 ounces / 794 g) can black beans, drained and rinsed
6 whole wheat buns

1. Make your bread crumbs using any leftover bread that you have. I used whole wheat but you could use sourdough and whatever else you prefer. Place bread in a food processor and process until the bread is a finely ground texture. Set aside. If you have any leftover bread crumbs, they can be frozen for 6 months. 2. Mix the chia seeds with 6 tablespoons water and set aside. 3. Heat 1 tablespoon oil (if desired) in a large skillet, add the onion and carrot, and sauté about 10 minutes. Add the corn and cook another 3 minutes. Add the spices and garlic to the onion and cook another minute. 4. Pat the black beans dry. You want to make sure they aren't wet when mashing and adding to the rest of ingredients. In a large bowl, add the black beans and mash with a potato masher or the back of a fork. You could pulse them in a food processor instead, but not too fine. Stir in the chia seed mixture. Mix in the onion mixture, bread crumbs, sunflower seed kernels, and hempseed. 5. Make into six patties. At this point you can freeze the patties, before frying. 6. Fry the patties in 1 tablespoon medium-hot oil (if desired) until browned on each side. 7. Serve on the whole wheat buns with your favorite toppings.

Per Serving

Calories: 310 | fat: 18g | protein: 22g | carbs: 31g | fiber: 7g

Sweet Potato Patties

Prep time: 15 minutes | Cook time: 20 minutes | Makes 5 to 6 patties

1 cup cooked short-grain brown rice, fully cooled
½ cup diced onion
¼ cup fresh parsley, finely chopped
1 to 2 tablespoons nutritional yeast (optional)
1 teaspoon olive oil (optional)
1 cup grated sweet potato
Pinch sea salt (optional)
1 tablespoon dried dill, or 2 tablespoons fresh
½ cup whole-grain flour, or bread crumbs, or gluten-free flour

1. Stir together the rice, sweet potato, onion, and salt (if using) in a large bowl. Allow it to sit for a few minutes, so that the salt can draw the moisture out of the potato and onion. Stir in the parsley, dill, and nutritional yeast (if using), then add enough flour to make the batter sticky, adding a spoonful or two of water if necessary. 2. Form the mixture into tight balls, and squish slightly into patties. 3. Heat a large skillet on medium, then add the oil (if using). Cook for 7 to 10 minutes, then flip. Cook another 5 to 7 minutes, and serve.

Per Serving (1 patty)

Calories: 115 | fat: 1g | protein: 3g | carbs: 23g | fiber: 2g

Burrito Bowl with Oil-Free Tortilla Chips

Prep time: 10 minutes | Cook time: 10 minutes | Serves 2

4 corn tortillas
1 cup cooked black beans
2 teaspoons chili powder
½ teaspoon garlic powder
2 cups shredded lettuce
¼ cup salsa
1 cup cooked brown rice
1 cup fresh or frozen corn
1 teaspoon ground cumin
½ teaspoon onion powder
1 avocado, peeled, pitted, and sliced

1. Preheat the oven to 350ºF (180ºC). Line a baking sheet with parchment paper. 2. Cut each tortilla into 6 evenly-sized chips, and place the chips on the baking sheet. Bake for 8 to 10 minutes, or until golden brown. The chips will continue to crisp up as they cool. 3. In a large bowl, combine the rice, black beans, corn, chili powder, cumin, garlic powder, and onion powder. If the rice and beans are cold, warm this mixture in the microwave on high for 2 minutes or on the stovetop in a medium saucepan over medium heat for 5 minutes. 4. Divide the warm rice, bean, and corn mixture into two serving bowls, then top each bowl with 1 cup of shredded lettuce and half of the avocado slices and salsa. 5. Serve with the crispy tortilla chips and any other condiment of your choosing.

Per Serving

Calories: 537 | fat: 17g | protein: 18g | carbs: 86g | fiber: 21g

Hawaiian-Inspired Pepper Pot with Brown Rice

Prep time: 15 minutes | Cook time: 2 to 3 hours | Serves 4 to 6

Nonstick cooking spray (optional)
1 medium red bell pepper, diced
1½ cups brown rice
1 (20-ounce / 567-g) can pineapple pieces in juice, undrained
2 tablespoons date syrup or maple syrup (optional)
1 teaspoon garlic powder
Ground black pepper
1 medium onion, diced
1 medium green bell pepper, diced
3 cups store-bought low-sodium vegetable broth
2 tablespoons low-sodium soy sauce, tamari, or coconut aminos
1 piece (1-inch) fresh ginger, peeled and minced, or 1 teaspoon ground ginger
Salt (optional)

1. Coat the inside of the slow cooker with cooking spray (if using) or line it with a slow cooker liner. 2. Add the onion, red and green bell peppers, rice, broth, pineapple, soy sauce, syrup (if using), ginger, garlic powder, black pepper, and salt (if using). Stir well to combine. 3. Cover and cook on High for 2 to 3 hours or on Low for 5 to 6 hours. Stir occasionally during the last hour of cooking to keep the rice from settling and overcooking.

Per Serving

Calories: 379 | fat: 3g | protein: 9g | carbs: 87g | fiber: 7g

Spiced Green Lentil Sandwich

Prep time: 15 minutes | Cook time: 30 minutes | Serves 8

1 cup green lentils
½ cup chopped onion
¾ cup old-fashioned oats
1 tablespoon hempseed, toasted in shell
4 tablespoons tamari
1½ teaspoons smoked paprika
¼ teaspoon ground black pepper
8 sandwich buns
1 small potato, to equal about ½ cup mashed potato
1 carrot, finely chopped in a processor
½ cup pepitas or sunflower seed kernels
1 cup bread crumbs
1 teaspoon ground ginger
½ teaspoon salt (optional)
1 tablespoon coconut oil (optional)

1. Place 2 cups water and the lentils in a large saucepan. Cover and bring to a boil. Turn down to low and cook for 20 minutes. Drain off remaining liquid from the lentils, if any. Set the lentils aside. 2. Pierce the potato a couple of times with a sharp knife. Wrap in a damp paper towel. Set in the microwave and cook on high for 4 minutes or until you can pinch the potato easily. Peel the potato and mash well. Set aside. 3. Heat 2 tablespoons water in a skillet over medium-high heat. Add the onion and sauté for 10 minutes. Remove from the heat. 4. Add the lentils, potato, onion, and the remainder of the ingredients to a large bowl (excluding the oil and the buns). Mix well. Form eight patties to the size of your sandwich buns. 5. Heat the oil (if desired) in a frying pan and fry the lentil patties on each side without crowding. 6. Spread the buns with all your favorite condiments and any other toppings of your choice. 7. You may also freeze extra patties for future meals.

Per Serving

Calories: 337 | fat: 16g | protein: 15g | carbs: 37g | fiber: 7g

Cajun-Style Jambalaya

Prep time: 15 minutes | Cook time: 3 to 4 hours | Serves 4 to 6

Nonstick cooking spray (optional)
1 medium green bell pepper, diced
4 garlic cloves, minced
1 (14½-ounce / 411-g) can kidney beans, drained and rinsed
2 cups uncooked brown rice
4 cups store-bought low-sodium vegetable broth
1 teaspoon dried oregano
½ teaspoon cayenne powder
Salt (optional)
1 medium onion, diced
3 celery stalks, diced
1 (14½-ounce / 411-g) can no-salt-added diced tomatoes
1 bay leaf
1 (8-ounce / 227-g) can tomato sauce
1 teaspoon dried thyme
2 teaspoons paprika
Ground black pepper

1. Coat the inside of the slow cooker with cooking spray (if using) or line it with a slow cooker liner. 2. Add the onion, bell pepper, celery, garlic, tomatoes, beans, bay leaf, rice, tomato sauce, broth, thyme, oregano, paprika, cayenne, black pepper, and salt (if using). 3. Cover and cook on High for 3 to 4 hours or on Low for 7 to 8 hours, stirring once per hour after the first two hours to avoid sticking. Remove and discard the bay leaf before serving.

Per Serving

Calories: 466 | fat: 4g | protein: 15g | carbs: 102g | fiber: 15g

Lentil Sloppy Joes

Prep time: 10 minutes | Cook time: 35 minutes | Serves 4

4 cups water, plus 1 tablespoon and more as needed, divided
1 teaspoon onion powder
1 teaspoon dried parsley
1 onion, diced
1 carrot, diced
1 tablespoon tamari
1 teaspoon apple cider vinegar
1 cup dried brown lentils
1 tablespoon paprika
1 teaspoon garlic powder
8 ounces (227 g) button mushrooms, chopped
1 red bell pepper, diced
4 ounces (113 g) tomato paste
1 tablespoon pure maple syrup (optional)
Multigrain bread, pita, whole wheat buns, or romaine lettuce leaves, for serving

1. In an 8-quart pot over high heat, bring 3 cups of water to a boil. Reduce the heat to maintain a simmer and add the lentils. Cover the pot and cook for 20 minutes, or until tender. Transfer the cooked lentils to a bowl. 2. In small bowl, stir together the paprika, onion powder, garlic powder, and parsley. Set aside. 3. Heat a pot over medium-high heat. Add the mushrooms and cook for 3 minutes to remove their moisture. Add the onion, red bell pepper, and carrot. Cook for 3 minutes more, or until the onion becomes translucent. Add water, 1 tablespoon at a time, to prevent burning. 4. Stir in the tomato paste and cook for 30 seconds. 5. Stir in the tamari, maple syrup (if using), and vinegar to combine. Stir in the spice mixture. Add the remaining 1 cup of water and stir to combine. 6. Stir in the cooked lentils, adding more water to thin, as desired. The mixture should be fairly thick. Serve on your choice of bread or wrapped in leafy greens.

Per Serving

Calories: 236 | fat: 2g | protein: 15g | carbs: 46g | fiber: 11g

Acadian Black Beans and Rice

Prep time: 15 minutes | Cook time: 40 minutes | Serves 6

1½ cups brown rice
1 tablespoon extra virgin olive oil (optional)
1 chopped green bell pepper
1 clove garlic, finely chopped
¼ cup diced tomatoes
1 teaspoon garlic powder
1 teaspoon thyme
½ teaspoon cayenne pepper
1 teaspoon salt (optional)
3½ cups low sodium vegetable broth
½ chopped yellow onion
2 (15 ounces / 425 g) cans black beans, drained and rinsed
1 teaspoon parsley
1 teaspoon onion powder
1 teaspoon oregano
¼ teaspoon ground black pepper

1. Cook the rice with vegetable broth for this recipe. 2. In a large skillet, heat the oil (if desired) to medium and then add the onion and bell pepper. Sauté until the onion becomes transparent, about 10 minutes. Add all the remaining ingredients (except the rice) to the large skillet with the onion and bell pepper. Cook for 10 minutes. Add the rice and heat through.

Per Serving

Calories: 291 | fat: 6g | protein: 16g | carbs: 52g | fiber: 7g

Green Pepper, Potato, and Mushroom Scallopini Sandwiches

Prep time: 15 minutes | Cook time: 2 to 3 hours | Makes 6 to 8 sandwiches

1 medium onion, diced
2 medium green bell peppers, cut into 1½-inch pieces
6 red or yellow potatoes (about 2 pounds / 907 g), unpeeled and cut into 1½-inch pieces
⅓ cup red wine or water
¼ teaspoon red pepper flakes (optional)
Salt (optional)
6 to 8 (6-inch) whole-grain sub rolls, for serving
4 garlic cloves, minced
1 pound (454 g) white button or cremini mushrooms, halved
1 (28-ounce / 794-g) can no-salt-added crushed tomatoes
1 tablespoon Italian seasoning
Ground black pepper
10 fresh basil leaves, torn, divided (optional)

1. Put the onion, garlic, bell peppers, mushrooms, potatoes, and tomatoes in the slow cooker. Swirl the red wine inside the empty tomato can and pour everything into the slow cooker. Add the Italian seasoning, red pepper flakes (if using), black pepper, and salt (if using). Stir to combine. 2. Cover and cook on High for 2 to 3 hours or on Low for 5 to 6 hours. Stir occasionally and add more water as needed while cooking to avoid sticking. 3. Before serving, stir in 6 torn basil leaves (if using). Portion about ½ cup of scallopini onto each roll, then top with the remaining 4 torn basil leaves.

Per Serving

Calories: 370 | fat: 2g | protein: 16g | carbs: 70g | fiber: 13g

Roasted Golden Beet Curry

Prep time: 15 minutes | Cook time: 1 hour | Serves 4

1 large golden beet, peeled and chopped into 1-inch pieces (about 4 cups)
4 cups no-sodium vegetable broth
1 tablespoon coconut aminos or tamari
2 teaspoons yellow curry powder
½ teaspoon ground turmeric
1 (14-ounce / 397-g) can full-fat coconut milk
1 onion, coarsely chopped
3 garlic cloves, peeled and stemmed
1 (12-ounce / 340-g) package silken tofu
1 tablespoon grated peeled fresh ginger, or 1 teaspoon ground ginger
¼ teaspoon cayenne pepper

1. Preheat the oven to 400°F (205°C). Line a baking sheet with parchment paper. 2. On the prepared baking sheet, spread the beet pieces in an even layer and top with the onion pieces and garlic cloves. 3. Bake for 45 minutes, until lightly browned and fork-tender. Transfer to a large pot and place it over medium heat. 4. Add the vegetable broth, tofu, coconut aminos, ginger, curry powder, turmeric, and cayenne pepper to the pot. Bring to a simmer. Cover the pot and cook for 15 minutes. 5. Add the coconut milk. Using an immersion blender, purée until smooth. Or transfer the soup to a blender, working in batches as needed, and blend until smooth. 6. Serve with rice or a grain and add a variety of cooked root vegetables and greens, as desired.

Per Serving

Calories: 259 | fat: 20g | protein: 7g | carbs: 18g | fiber: 3g

Falafel Burgers

Prep time: 15 minutes | Cook time: 30 minutes | Serves 8

3 cups cooked chickpeas
¼ cup vegetable broth
1 tablespoon freshly squeezed lemon juice
2 teaspoons onion powder
1 teaspoon ground coriander
Whole-wheat buns
2 cups cooked brown rice
¼ cup chopped fresh parsley
2 teaspoons garlic powder
1½ teaspoons ground cumin
¼ teaspoon freshly ground black pepper
Lettuce, tomato, and onion, for topping (optional)

1. Preheat the oven to 425°F (220°C). Line a baking sheet with parchment paper. 2. In a food processor or blender, combine the chickpeas, rice, broth, parsley, lemon juice, garlic powder, onion powder, cumin, coriander, and pepper. Process on low for 30 to 45 seconds, or until the mixture can easily be formed into patties but isn't so well mixed that you create hummus. You may need to stop the processor and scrape down the sides once or twice. 3. Scoop out ½ cup of the chickpea mixture, and form it into a patty. Place the patty on the baking sheet. Repeat until all of the chickpea mixture is used. 4. Bake for 15 minutes. Flip the patties, cook for 12 to 15 minutes more, and serve on buns with your preferred toppings.

Per Serving

Calories: 230 | fat: 3g | protein: 10g | carbs: 44g | fiber: 8g

Broccoli and Mushroom Stir-Fry

Prep time: 10 minutes | Cook time: 25 minutes | Serves 4

¼ cup soy sauce
2 tablespoons seasoned rice vinegar
¼ teaspoon ground ginger
2 teaspoons cornstarch
3 scallions, green and white parts, thinly sliced (about ½ cup)
3 cups (1-inch) broccoli florets
Sesame seeds, for garnish
¼ cup water, plus 5 tablespoons, divided
½ teaspoon garlic powder
¼ to ½ teaspoon red pepper flakes
2 (8-ounce / 227-g) containers sliced cremini mushrooms
1 cup sliced (¼-inch-thick) carrots
4 to 6 cups cooked brown rice

1. In a small bowl, whisk together the soy sauce, ¼ cup of water, the vinegar, garlic powder, ginger, red pepper flakes, and cornstarch. 2. In a large sauté pan or skillet, combine the mushrooms, scallions, and 1 tablespoon of water. Sauté over high heat, stirring occasionally, for about 10 minutes, or until the mushrooms have browned and most of the liquid has evaporated. Transfer to a dish. 3. Return the pan to the stove. Still over high heat, add the carrots and 2 tablespoons of water. Cook, stirring occasionally, for 3 minutes, or until slightly softened. 4. Stir in the broccoli and remaining 2 tablespoons of water. Cook (adding a tablespoon of water as necessary to prevent burning) for about 6 minutes, or until the broccoli is bright green and crisp-tender and the liquid has evaporated. 5. Return the mushrooms with their liquid to the pan. 6. Stir in the soy sauce mixture, and cook for 1 to 2 minutes, or until the sauce thickens. Remove from the heat. 7. Serve the stir-fry over the brown rice, and garnish with sesame seeds.

Per Serving

Calories: 364 | fat: 3g | protein: 11g | carbs: 73g | fiber: 5g

Broccoli Spinach Stuffed Baguette

Prep time: 25 minutes | Cook time: 25 minutes | Serves 2

Vegetables:

2 cups broccoli florets
2 cloves garlic, finely diced
1 tablespoon extra virgin olive oil (optional)
5 ounces (142 g) baby spinach, chopped, with the long stems cut away and discarded

Cashew Cheese:

½ cup raw cashews, soaked 1 hour and drained
1½ tablespoons nutritional yeast
½ teaspoon salt (optional)
1 cup water
4 tablespoons tapioca starch
½ teaspoon garlic powder

Assemble:

1 baguette
2 tablespoons raw shelled hempseed
1 ounce (28 g) grape tomatoes, sliced thin

Make Vegetables: 1. Add water to a medium saucepan with a steamer insert and bring to a boil. Add the broccoli to the insert and steam over boiling water for 10 minutes. Remove from steamer and set aside. 2. Heat the oil (if desired) in a large skillet over medium-high heat. Use a skillet that has a lid. Add the garlic and cook for 1 minute. Add the spinach, toss, and cook for 1 minute. Cover and let sit for 2 minutes. 3. Add the broccoli and spinach to a large bowl. Make Cashew Cheese: 4. Add all of the cashew cheese ingredients to a blender and blend until completely smooth. 5. Pour into a small saucepan and bring heat up to medium high. Keep cooking and stirring until it goes through its thickening process and becomes a gooey, cheesy sauce. This takes 5 to 10 minutes. 6. Add to the bowl with the broccoli mixture. Stir well. Assemble: 7. Cut off the top of the baguette and scoop out some of the bread from the center using a spoon. Make sure you leave an edge of bread in the shell to help hold the filling. 8. Spoon the broccoli-cheese mixture down the center of the baguette. Top with sliced grape tomatoes and sprinkle with hempseed. Cut in half. You could also cut into slices and serve as an appetizer.

Per Serving

Calories: 365 | fat: 14g | protein: 32g | carbs: 48g | fiber: 6g

Chapter 5 Pizzas, Wraps, and Sandwiches

"The Game Changer" Burger

Prep time: 5 minutes | Cook time: 15 minutes | Makes 4 patties

¾ cup walnuts, soaked in water for 8 hours or overnight
½ sweet onion, chopped
1 cup mushrooms, washed and chopped
1 tablespoon ground flaxseeds
¼ teaspoon freshly ground pepper
1 tablespoon coconut aminos or nama shoyu
1 tablespoon coconut oil, plus more to cook patties (optional)
2 cloves garlic, minced
½ (8-ounce / 227-g) package tempeh, crumbled
¼ teaspoon sea salt (optional)
½ teaspoon smoked paprika
½ cup shredded beet

1. Drain and rinse the soaked walnuts; set aside. 2. Heat a medium skillet over medium heat. Once hot, add the oil (if using), onion, garlic and mushrooms and sauté for 3 to 4 minutes, or until the onion is fragrant, soft and translucent. Remove from the heat and transfer the mixture to a food processor or blender. Add the walnuts, tempeh, flaxseeds, salt (if using), pepper, smoked paprika and coconut aminos. Process until well combined but still grainy. 3. Transfer the mixture to a large bowl and mix in the shredded beet. Set aside for about 15 minutes, so the flax can soak up the liquid and the mixture sets (this step is important for the patties to hold together). 4. Lightly oil a medium skillet with coconut oil and heat over medium heat. 5. Meanwhile, shape the burger mixture into 4 patties and arrange as many as you can in the skillet without overcrowding. Cook the patties for about 4 minutes on each side, until lightly browned. Cook any remaining patties in the same manner.

Per Serving

Calories: 298 | fat: 22g | protein: 15g | carbs: 14g | fiber: 3g

Smashed White Bean Salad Sammies

Prep time: 15 minutes | Cook time: 0 minutes | Makes 2 sandwiches

1 garlic clove, minced
1 scallion, greens and white parts, minced
1 (15-ounce / 425-g) can cannellini beans, drained and rinsed
2 tablespoons tahini
Pinch of salt, plus more as needed (optional)
4 slices whole-grain bread
1 medium tomato, sliced
2 tablespoons minced celery (about ½ stalk)
2 or 3 fresh mint leaves, finely chopped
Juice of ½ large lemon

Pinch ground cumin
Pinch red pepper flakes
1 handful arugula

1. In a large bowl, mix together the garlic, celery, scallion, and mint. Add the drained beans, lemon juice, tahini, cumin, salt (if using), and red pepper flakes and stir, mashing the beans with a fork, until combined. The mixture will be rustic and chunky. 2. To make each sandwich, spread about ½ cup of filling onto 1 slice of bread, top with arugula and tomato slices, sprinkle with a little salt (if desired), and top with another piece of bread. Refrigerate leftover filling for up to 4 days.

Per Serving

Calories: 397 | fat: 12g | protein: 20g | carbs: 57g | fiber: 7g

Brown Rice and Black Bean Veggie Burgers

Prep time: 15 minutes | Cook time: 20 minutes | Makes 6 patties

1 cup water
Olive oil cooking spray
1 (15-ounce / 425-g) can black beans, drained and rinsed
1 tablespoon garlic powder
½ teaspoon smoked paprika
1 teaspoon ground flaxseeds
¼ teaspoon salt (optional)
1 sweet potato, peeled and cut into ½-inch pieces (about 1 cup)
1½ cups frozen brown rice
1 tablespoon onion powder
1 teaspoon tapioca flour
1 tablespoon nutritional yeast
4 whole-wheat burger buns, for serving

1. In a medium saucepan, bring the water to a boil over high heat. Add the sweet potato and cook until it's easily pierced with a fork, about 10 minutes. Drain and set aside to cool. 2. Preheat the oven to 425°F (220°C). Spray a sheet pan with olive oil cooking spray. 3. In a large bowl, combine the sweet potato and black beans and, using a fork or potato masher, mash until they are well combined but still chunky. Add the frozen rice, garlic powder, onion powder, smoked paprika, tapioca flour, ground flaxseeds, nutritional yeast, and salt (if using) and mix until well combined. The mixture will be very sticky. 4. Using your hands, form the mixture into 6 equal patties. Put the patties onto the prepared sheet pan and bake for 10 minutes. Flip the burgers and continue to bake for another 10 minutes, until browned and crispy. Arrange on buns and serve.

Per Serving

Calories: 142 | fat: 1g | protein: 6g | carbs: 28g | fiber: 6g

Spiced Eggplant and Hummus Sandwiches

Prep time: 10 minutes | Cook time: 20 minutes | Makes 2 sandwiches

1 (½-pound / 227-g) Italian eggplant, cut lengthwise into 4 slices
½ teaspoon smoked paprika
2 red or yellow bell peppers, seeded and halved
¼ cup store-bought hummus
1 medium tomato, cut into thick slices
½ teaspoon salt, plus more for the eggplant
1 tablespoon extra-virgin olive oil (optional)
½ teaspoon garlic powder
4 slices whole-wheat bread
1 cup arugula
2 tablespoons sesame seeds (optional)

1. Preheat the oven to 425°F (220°C). 2. Arrange the eggplant slices on a sheet pan and salt (if using) lightly. Let sit for 10 minutes until they release their juices, then rinse the slices and pat dry. Using a sharp knife, score the eggplant slices in a crosshatch pattern. Set aside. 3. In a large bowl, mix together the oil, ½ teaspoon salt, smoked paprika, and garlic powder to make a wet rub. Dredge the eggplant slices in the rub, making sure they are coated well. Arrange them on the sheet pan in a single layer with the crosshatch side up. 4. Arrange the bell peppers around the eggplant and bake for 10 minutes. Using tongs or a spatula, flip the eggplant and continue to bake for another 10 minutes. 5. When the vegetables are almost done, toast the bread. To assemble the sandwiches, spread the hummus in a thick layer on a slice of toast, add half of the arugula, tomatoes, eggplant, and peppers, sprinkle with sesame seeds (if using), and top with a second slice of toast. Repeat for the second sandwich.

Per Serving

Calories: 357 | fat: 12g | protein: 13g | carbs: 51g | fiber: 12g

Rice and Bean Veggie Burgers

Prep time: 15 minutes | Cook time: 45 minutes | Serves 8

1 cup uncooked medium-grain brown rice
5 cloves garlic, peeled
½ cup grated carrots
2 tablespoons nutritional yeast
2 teaspoons arrowroot powder
¼ cup chopped fresh leafy herbs of your choice
4 teaspoons gluten-free tamari soy sauce
Salt and pepper, to taste (optional)
½ cup raw sunflower seeds
¾ cup chopped red onion
¾ cup cooked and drained beans of choice
2 tablespoons certified gluten-free oat flour
4 teaspoons ground spices of choice
2 tablespoons tomato paste
1 to 2 tablespoons filtered water

1. Place the rice in a medium saucepan, and cover it with 2 cups of filtered water. Bring to a boil over medium heat. Lower the heat to a simmer and cook the rice for 15 minutes. It should still be quite chewy but not hard. Drain the rice if necessary, and scrape into a large bowl. Set aside. 2. In a food processor, combine the sunflower seeds, garlic, red onions, grated carrots, and beans. Pulse the machine until you have a chunky paste. Add this paste into the large bowl with the rice. 3. To the rice and paste mixture, add the nutritional yeast, oat flour, arrowroot powder, spices, herbs, tomato paste, tamari, 1 tablespoon of the filtered water, salt, and pepper, if using. Mix everything with your hands until the mixture holds together when you pinch it. Add more filtered water if necessary. 4. Form the mixture into 8 equal patties. Refrigerate the patties for at least 1 hour so that they can properly set. 5. Preheat the oven to 350°F (180°C). 6. Remove the patties from the refrigerator, and place them on a baking sheet. Bake the veggie burgers for 30 minutes, flipping them at the halfway point. They should be evenly browned, lightly crispy at the edges, and firm. Serve veggie burgers hot with accompaniments.

Per Serving

Calories: 177 | fat: 6g | protein: 6g | carbs: 27g | fiber: 3g

Grilled Zucchini and Hummus Wrap

Prep time: 15 minutes | Cook time: 6 minutes | Serves 2

1 zucchini, ends removed, thinly sliced lengthwise
¼ teaspoon freshly ground black pepper
¼ cup hummus
2 Roma tomatoes, cut lengthwise into slices
2 tablespoons chopped red onion
½ teaspoon dried oregano
¼ teaspoon garlic powder
2 whole wheat tortillas
1 cup chopped kale
½ teaspoon ground cumin

1. In a skillet over medium heat, place the zucchini slices and cook for 3 minutes per side. Sprinkle with the oregano, pepper, and garlic powder and remove from the heat. 2. Spread 2 tablespoons of hummus on each tortilla. Lay half the zucchini in the center of each tortilla. Top with tomato slices, kale, red onion, and ¼ teaspoon of cumin. Wrap tightly and enjoy.

Per Serving

Calories: 247 | fat: 8g | protein: 9g | carbs: 37g | fiber: 8g

Garden Burgers

Prep time: 15 minutes | Cook time: 30 minutes | Serves 6

1 cup gluten-free rolled oats
1 yellow onion, diced
½ cup shredded carrots
1 (15-ounce / 425-g) can black beans, drained and rinsed
¼ cup oil-packed sun-dried tomatoes, drained and chopped
1 teaspoon chili powder
¼ teaspoon ground black pepper
1 tablespoon avocado oil, plus more for cooking (optional)
4 garlic cloves, halved
½ cup fresh parsley, stems removed
½ cup sunflower seeds, toasted
1 teaspoon ground cumin
1 teaspoon paprika
¾ teaspoon sea salt (optional)
¼ teaspoon ground red pepper

For Serving:

2 ripe avocados, sliced
1 cup sprouts or microgreens
1 ripe tomato, sliced
6 gluten-free or whole wheat buns, split in half and toasted, or 6 leaves romaine lettuce

1. In a food processor, pulse the oats until coarsely chopped. Set aside. 2. Heat 1 tablespoon oil (if using) in a skillet. Add the onion and carrots and cook for 10 minutes, or until softened. Add the garlic and cook for 30 seconds. 3. Transfer the onion mixture to the food processor with the oats. Add the beans and remaining ingredients. Pulse until everything is finely chopped and holds together but not puréed. 4. Line a baking sheet or plate with parchment paper. Form 6 equally sized patties that are about 4 inches in diameter and ½ inch thick. Cover the patties and refrigerate or freeze them until firm. 5. Heat a few tablespoons of oil (if using) in a nonstick skillet on medium-high heat. Place the patties in the pan, working in batches if needed. Cook for 5 minutes, then carefully flip. Cook for an additional 10 minutes, or until golden and crispy on the edges. (Frozen burgers will need a few extra minutes.) Serve with desired toppings on buns or as a lettuce wrap.

Per Serving

Calories: 288 | fat: 20g | protein: 8g | carbs: 35g | fiber: 11g

Chickpea Curry Salad Sandwiches

Prep time: 10 minutes | Cook time: 0 minutes | Makes 2 sandwiches

1 (15-ounce / 425-g) can chickpeas, drained and rinsed
Juice of ½ lemon
½ cup raisins
¼ teaspoon salt (optional)
2 teaspoons store-bought plant-based mayonnaise
1 apple, cored and chopped in small cubes
1 celery stalk, finely chopped
1 teaspoon curry powder
4 slices whole-wheat bread

1. In a large bowl, mash the chickpeas with the back of a fork. They will break into pieces and get crumbly but not mushy. Add the mayonnaise and mix until well combined. 2. Add the apple, lemon juice, celery, raisins, curry powder, and salt (if using) and mix well. Taste and adjust the seasonings, if desired. Sandwich about ¼ cup of filling between 2 slices of bread.

Per Serving

Calories: 489 | fat: 7g | protein: 18g | carbs: 94g | fiber: 15g

Maple Dijon Burgers

Prep time: 10 minutes | Cook time: 30 minutes | Makes 12 burgers

1 red bell pepper
1 cup ground almonds
2 teaspoons Dijon mustard
1 garlic clove, pressed
1 teaspoon dried oregano
1 cup spinach
1 (19-ounce / 539-g) can chickpeas, rinsed and drained, or 2 cups cooked
2 teaspoons maple syrup (optional)
Juice of ½ lemon
½ teaspoon dried sage
1 to 1½ cups rolled oats

1. Preheat the oven to 350°F (180°C). Line a large baking sheet with parchment paper. 2. Cut the red pepper in half, remove the stem and seeds, and put on the baking sheet cut side up in the oven. Roast in the oven while you prep the other ingredients. 3. Put the chickpeas in the food processor, along with the almonds, mustard, maple syrup (if using), garlic, lemon juice, oregano, sage, and spinach. Pulse until things are thoroughly combined but not puréed. When the red pepper is softened a bit, about 10 minutes, add it to the processor along with the oats and pulse until they are chopped just enough to form patties. 4. If you don't have a food processor, mash the chickpeas with a potato masher or fork, and make sure everything else is chopped up as finely as possible, then stir together. 5. Scoop up ¼-cup portions and form into 12 patties, and lay them out on the baking sheet. 6. Put the burgers in the oven and bake until the outside is lightly browned, about 30 minutes.

Per Serving (1 burger)
Calories: 101 | fat: 5g | protein: 4g | carbs: 13g | fiber: 3g

Curried Mango Chickpea Wrap

Prep time: 15 minutes | Cook time: 0 minutes | Makes 3 wraps

3 tablespoons tahini
1 tablespoon curry powder
3 to 4 tablespoons water
1 cup diced mango
1 red bell pepper, seeded and diced small
3 large whole-grain wraps
Zest and juice of 1 lime
¼ teaspoon sea salt (optional)
1 (14-ounce / 397-g) can chickpeas, rinsed and drained, or 1½ cups cooked
½ cup fresh cilantro, chopped
1 to 2 cups shredded green leaf lettuce

1. In a medium bowl, whisk together the tahini, lime zest and juice, curry powder, and salt (if using) until the mixture is creamy and thick. Add 3 to 4 tablespoons water to thin it out a bit. Or you can process this all in a blender. The taste should be strong and salty, to flavor the whole salad. 2. Toss the chickpeas, mango, bell pepper, and cilantro with the tahini dressing. 3. Spoon the salad down the center of the wraps, top with shredded lettuce, and then roll up and enjoy.

Per Serving (1 wrap)
Calories: 256 | fat: 10g | protein: 9g | carbs: 34g | fiber: 8g

Rainbow Collard Wraps

Prep time: 20 minutes | Cook time: 0 minutes | Serves 4

¼ cup smooth peanut butter
1 tablespoon coconut aminos
½ teaspoon garlic powder
½ cup hummus
1 English cucumber, cut into matchsticks
1 celery stalk, cut into thin strips
2 avocados, pitted and thickly cut
2 tablespoons rice vinegar
1 tablespoon minced peeled fresh ginger
4 large collard green leaves
4 carrots, cut into matchsticks
1 red bell pepper, cut into thin strips
1 small red cabbage, cut into strips
1 cup chopped fresh cilantro

1. In a small bowl, whisk together the peanut butter, vinegar, coconut aminos, ginger, and garlic powder to blend. Set aside. 2. Bring an 8-quart pot of water to a boil over high heat. Drop each collard green leaf in the water for 30 seconds. Transfer to a clean kitchen towel and pat dry. Using a sharp kitchen knife, trim the thick, tough rib of each collard green leaf, cutting it so the stem is flush with the rest of the leaf, rather than cutting out the stem completely. 3. Spread 2 tablespoons of hummus down the center of each prepared leaf. Place one-quarter of the carrots, cucumber, bell pepper, celery, red cabbage, and avocados on top of the hummus. Top with a sprinkle of cilantro and a drizzle of peanut butter sauce. 4. Fold each leaf like a burrito, rolling it and folding in the sides to contain the vegetables and filling. Roll the wraps tightly so they are easier to enjoy. Halve and serve.

Per Serving

Calories: 378 | fat: 23g | protein: 11g | carbs: 37g | fiber: 14g

Chickpea Gyros

Prep time: 15 minutes | Cook time: 20 minutes | Serves 4

1 tablespoon paprika
1 teaspoon dried oregano
¼ teaspoon cayenne pepper
1 (15-ounce /425-g) can chickpeas, drained and rinsed
¼ cup finely chopped cucumber
¼ cup chopped tomato
1 teaspoon freshly ground black pepper
½ teaspoon garlic powder
¼ teaspoon onion powder
1 cup hummus
4 whole wheat pitas
¼ cup red onion strips
2 romaine lettuce leaves, finely chopped

1. Preheat the oven to 400°F (205°C). Line a baking sheet with parchment paper. 2. In a medium bowl, stir together the paprika, black pepper, oregano, garlic powder, cayenne pepper, and onion powder. Add the chickpeas and toss to coat. Spread the chickpeas into a single layer on the prepared baking sheet. 3. Bake for 10 minutes. Stir and flip the chickpeas and bake for 10 minutes more, until slightly crispy (they will become crispier as they cool). Remove from the oven and let cool on the baking sheet. 4. Spread ¼ cup of hummus on each pita. Top each with one-quarter of the roasted chickpeas, 1 tablespoon each of the cucumber, red onion, and tomato, and one-quarter of the lettuce. Fold and enjoy.

Per Serving

Calories: 400 | fat: 11g | protein: 15g | carbs: 61g | fiber: 13g

Stacked N' Spicy Portobello Burgers

Prep time: 20 minutes | Cook time: 25 minutes | Serves 2

1 (8-ounce / 227-g) block firm tofu, drained
4 large portobello mushroom caps, stems removed
½ green bell pepper, pitted and diced
3 cups fresh spinach, rinsed and dried
4 tablespoons hummus
1 tablespoon taco seasoning
¼ teaspoon chili powder
1 tablespoon extra virgin olive oil (optional)
1 large onion, diced
½ red bell pepper, pitted and diced
2 whole wheat vegan buns
¼ cup salsa
½ teaspoon paprika

1. Cut the tofu into 4 large slices and set aside. Heat the olive oil in a large skillet over medium-high heat. Add the mushroom caps and flip them over after 4 minutes of cooking. Sprinkle the caps with the taco seasoning, paprika, chili powder, and salt. Flip again after 4 minutes, allowing them to cook until they have halved in size. Remove the caps from the skillet and set aside. 2. Add the tofu slices to the previously used skillet and cook them on both sides until slightly brown; set them aside. Add the diced onions and bell peppers to the skillet. Stir frequently and cook the vegetables until browned, for 10 to 12 minutes. Turn the heat down to low and add the mushrooms back to the skillet, and reheat for 2 more minutes. 3. Spread hummus on one side of each bun, and the salsa on the other half. Top the hummus with a handful of spinach and serve with two mushroom caps, tofu squares, and top with a heaping scoop of vegetables with more salt to taste. 4. Enjoy the portobello burgers right away, or store and serve later!

Per Serving

Calories: 421 | fat: 16g | protein: 21g | carbs: 49g | fiber: 10g

BBQ Jackfruit Sandwiches

Prep time: 5 minutes | Cook time: 30 minutes | Serves 2

1 (15-ounce / 425-g) can jackfruit, drained and shredded
2 garlic cloves, finely chopped
1 tablespoon molasses
3 tablespoons tomato paste
½ teaspoon salt (optional)
2 whole-wheat burger buns
2 teaspoons extra-virgin olive oil (optional)
½ medium yellow onion, finely chopped
2 teaspoons maple syrup (optional)
1 teaspoon apple cider vinegar
1 teaspoon smoked paprika
½ cup water
1 cup store-bought coleslaw

1. Preheat the oven to 400°F (205°C). 2. In an 8-by-8-inch baking dish, combine the jackfruit, olive oil, onion, and garlic and bake for 10 minutes. Using a spatula, turn the jackfruit and continue to bake for 10 more minutes. 3. In a small bowl, mix together the maple syrup, molasses, apple cider vinegar, tomato paste, smoked paprika, salt (if using), and water. Add the sauce to the jackfruit, mix well, and bake for 10 more minutes 4. To serve, pile the barbecue jackfruit on the buns and top with the slaw.

Per Serving

Calories: 430 | fat: 8g | protein: 10g | carbs: 88g | fiber: 7g

Apple-Tahini Sandwich

Prep time: 5 minutes | Cook time: 0 minutes | Serves 1

1 medium apple (organic if possible)
1 tablespoon hemp hearts
2 tablespoons raw tahini
Ground cinnamon

1. Wash, core and slice the apple into 6 rounds. (If you don't have an apple corer, you can slice the apple first and then cut out the centers with a small cookie cutter or knife.) 2. Spread the tahini on 3 of the apple slices and sprinkle with the hemp hearts and a little bit of cinnamon. Top with the remaining apple slices to form sandwiches.

Per Serving

Calories: 277 | fat: 14g | protein: 6g | carbs: 35g | fiber: 7g

Chapter 6 Salads

Peaches, Peas, and Beans Summer Salad

Prep time: 15 minutes | Cook time: 5 minutes | Serves 6

Dressing:

1 tablespoon balsamic vinegar
1 teaspoon gluten-free tamari soy sauce
Salt and pepper, to taste (optional)
1 teaspoon Dijon mustard
2 tablespoons coconut oil (optional)

Salad:

¾ pound (340 g) young green, yellow or burgundy string beans, trimmed
Large handful of snap peas, trimmed and sliced down the middle
¼ cup whole toasted almonds, coarsely chopped
2 ripe and firm peaches
1 small shallot, peeled and sliced paper thin
Salt and pepper, to taste (optional)
¼ cup chopped fresh basil leaves

1. Make the Dressing: In a small jar with a tight-fitting lid, combine the balsamic vinegar, Dijon mustard, tamari, oil, salt, and pepper, if using. Tightly secure the lid, and shake the jar vigorously until the dressing has a smooth consistency. Set aside. 2. Make the Salad: Bring a medium saucepan of water to a boil. Salt the water and then throw in the trimmed green beans. Blanch the beans for 3 minutes or until tender and crisp. Drain the beans and place them in a bowl of ice water to cool immediately. 3. Remove the pits from the peaches and cut the fruit into thin slices. In a large bowl, combine the sliced peaches, shallots, and snap peas. Drain the green beans and lightly dry them. Add the beans to the large bowl. Season the salad with salt and pepper, if using. 4. Pour the dressing over the vegetables and peaches, and toss lightly to combine. Scatter the chopped basil and almonds over the top, and serve.

Per Serving

Calories: 132 | fat: 8g | protein: 4g | carbs: 13g | fiber: 4g

Quinoa, Corn and Black Bean Salad

Prep time: 25 minutes | Cook time: 0 minutes | Serves 4

2½ cups cooked quinoa
1 red bell pepper, roasted, seeded, and diced
2 cups cooked black beans, or 1 (15-ounce / 425-g) can, drained and rinsed
1 jalapeño pepper, minced (for less heat, remove the seeds)
Salt, to taste (optional)
3 ears corn, kernels removed (about 2 cups)
½ small red onion, peeled and diced
1 cup finely chopped cilantro
6 green onions (white and green parts), thinly sliced
Zest of 1 lime and juice of 2 limes
1 tablespoon cumin seeds, toasted and ground

1. Combine all ingredients in a large bowl and mix well. Chill for 1 hour before serving

Per Serving

Calories: 366 | fat: 3g | protein: 16g | carbs: 70g | fiber: 14g

Bulgur Lettuce Cups

Prep time: 10 minutes | Cook time: 20 minutes | Serves 2 to 4

Sauce:

½ cup unsweetened natural peanut butter
3 tablespoons seasoned rice vinegar
1 teaspoon liquid aminos
¼ cup soy sauce
2 tablespoons lime juice
1 teaspoon sriracha

Cups:

1 cup bulgur
¼ cup seasoned rice vinegar
½ teaspoon ground ginger
1 cup shredded carrots
½ cup sliced scallions, green and white parts
½ cup soy sauce
½ teaspoon garlic powder
¼ teaspoon red pepper flakes
1 cup shredded cabbage
1 head red leaf lettuce or Bibb lettuce

Make the Sauce: 1. In a small bowl, combine the peanut butter, soy sauce, vinegar, lime juice, liquid aminos, and sriracha. Whisk until well combined. Make the Cups: 2. In a medium saucepan, cook the bulgur for about 12 minutes. Remove from the heat. Drain any excess water after cooking. 3. In a small bowl, combine the soy sauce, vinegar, garlic powder, ginger, and red pepper flakes. Mix well. 4. Add the carrots, cabbage, scallions, and soy sauce mixture to the cooked bulgur. Mix thoroughly. 5. Serve the filling scooped into individual lettuce leaves, topped with a drizzle of peanut sauce.

Per ServingCalories: 532 | fat: 17g | protein: 25g | carbs: 79g | fiber: 18g

Lentil, Lemon and Mushroom Salad

Prep time: 10 minutes | Cook time: 25 minutes | Serves 2

½ cup dry lentils of choice
3 cups mushrooms, thickly sliced
4 teaspoons extra virgin olive oil (optional)
¼ teaspoon chili flakes
2 tablespoons cilantro, chopped
Salt and pepper to taste (optional)
2 cups vegetable broth
1 cup sweet or purple onion, chopped
2 tablespoons garlic powder or 3 garlic cloves, minced
1 tablespoon lemon juice
½ cup arugula

1. Sprout the lentils for 2 to 3 days. 2. Place the vegetable stock in a deep saucepan and bring it to a boil. Add the lentils to the boiling broth, cover the pan, and cook for about 5 minutes over low heat until the lentils are a bit tender. Remove the pan from heat and drain the excess water. 3. Put a frying pan over high heat and add 2 tablespoons of olive oil. Add the onions, garlic, and chili flakes, and cook until the onions are almost translucent, around 5 to 10 minutes while stirring. Add the mushrooms to the frying pan and mix in thoroughly. Continue cooking until the onions are completely translucent and the mushrooms have softened; remove the pan from the heat. Mix the lentils, onions, mushrooms, and garlic in a large bowl. Add the lemon juice and the remaining olive oil. Toss or stir to combine everything thoroughly. 4. Serve the mushroom and onion mixture over some arugala in bowl, adding salt and pepper to taste, if desired, or, store and enjoy later!

Per Serving

Calories: 262 | fat: 10g | protein: 16g | carbs: 28g | fiber: 15g

Zingy Melon and Mango Salad

Prep time: 5 minutes | Cook time: 0 minutes | Serves 2

1 large mango, peeled, pitted, and cut into 1-inch pieces (about 1 cup)
Juice of 1 lime
1 teaspoon chili powder
½ small cantaloupe or watermelon, peeled and cut into 1-inch pieces (about 2 cups)
¼ cup chopped fresh cilantro

1. In a large bowl, combine the mango and cantaloupe. Add the lime juice and cilantro and gently toss until combined. To serve, spoon into bowls and sprinkle with chili powder.

Per Serving

Calories: 171 | fat: 1g | protein: 3g | carbs: 42g | fiber: 5g

Shaved Root Salad with Crispy Lentils

Prep time: 20 minutes | Cook time: 30 minutes | Serves 6

Dressing:

2 tablespoons virgin olive oil (optional)
1 tablespoon grainy mustard
1 tablespoon sherry vinegar or apple cider vinegar
1 clove garlic, grated
1 tablespoon pure maple syrup (optional)
1 tablespoon filtered water
1 teaspoon prepared horseradish
Salt and pepper, to taste (optional)

Salad:

⅓ cup French or black beluga lentils, rinsed
Salt and pepper, to taste (optional)
2 medium carrots, peeled
2 tablespoons chopped fresh dill, for garnish
½ teaspoon virgin olive oil (optional)
2 small beets, peeled
1 small celery root, peeled

1. Preheat the oven to 400°F (205°C). 2. Make the Dressing: In a jar with a tight-fitting lid, combine the olive oil, maple syrup, mustard, water, sherry vinegar, horseradish, garlic, salt, and pepper, if using. Tightly secure the lid, and shake the jar vigorously until the dressing has a creamy and smooth consistency. Set aside. 3. Make the Salad: Bring a medium saucepan of water to a boil. Drop in the lentils and a big pinch of salt, if using. Bring to a boil again, and then reduce heat to a simmer until lentils are just tender, about 20 minutes. Drain the lentils and spread them out on a kitchen towel to dry. 4. Transfer the dried lentils to a baking sheet. Toss the lentils with the olive oil, salt, and pepper, if using. Slide the baking sheet into the oven, and roast the lentils until they have dried and browned slightly, about 8 minutes. Remove from the oven and set aside. 5. Using a mandoline, slice the beets paper thin and place them in a large bowl. Slice the carrots with the mandoline, and add them to the bowl. Cut the celery root down the middle lengthwise. Slice each half of the celery root with the mandoline, and add the slices to the bowl. 6. Season all the sliced vegetables with salt and pepper, if using, and toss. 7. Toss the sliced vegetables with ⅔ of the dressing. Transfer the dressed vegetables to a serving platter. Scatter the crispy lentils over the vegetables. Pour the remaining dressing over the lentils. Garnish the salad with the fresh dill, and serve immediately.

Per Serving

Calories: 80 | fat: 5g | protein: 1g | carbs: 8g | fiber: 2g

Thanksgiving Panzanella Salad with Delicata Squash

Prep time: 25 minutes | Cook time: 50 minutes | Serves 6

Dressing:

2 tablespoons balsamic vinegar
1 small clove garlic, finely minced or grated
2 teaspoons pure maple syrup (optional)
Salt and pepper, to taste
1 teaspoon Dijon mustard
¼ cup plus 1 tablespoon virgin olive oil (optional)

Salad:

1 standard delicata squash
1 tablespoon plus 2 teaspoons virgin olive oil, divided (optional)
Salt and pepper, to taste (optional)
2 cups sliced Lacinato kale
2 stalks celery, thinly sliced
2 to 3 shallots, peeled
1 tablespoon minced fresh rosemary
2 teaspoons minced fresh thyme leaves
4 cups cubed whole-grain sourdough bread
⅓ cup pomegranate seeds
¼ cup leaves from the heart of a celery bunch or flat-leaf parsley, for garnish

1. Preheat the oven to 400°F (205°C). Line two baking sheets with parchment paper and set aside. 2. Make the Dressing: In a medium bowl, whisk together the balsamic vinegar, salt, pepper, if using, minced garlic, Dijon mustard, maple syrup, and olive oil, if using. Set aside. 3. Make the Salad: Cut the delicata squash down the middle lengthwise. Scoop out the seeds and discard them. Cut the squash halves into ¼-inch slices, and then transfer those slices to one of the parchment-lined baking sheets. 4. Cut the shallots into ½-inch wedges, trying to preserve the root end for intact pieces. Place them on the baking sheet with the delicata squash. 5. Right on the baking sheet, toss the squash and shallots with the 1 tablespoon of olive oil and the minced rosemary, thyme, salt, and pepper, if using. Once the vegetables are evenly coated, slide the baking sheet into the oven. Roast the squash and shallots for approximately 45 minutes, stirring and flipping the vegetables a couple of times, or until all pieces are golden brown and soft. Let the vegetables cool completely. 6. While the vegetables are roasting, transfer the bread cubes to the other parchment-lined baking sheet. Toss the bread cubes with the remaining 2 teaspoons of olive oil and the salt and pepper, if using. Once the bread is evenly coated, slide the baking sheet into the oven. Bake the bread pieces, stirring and flipping a couple of times, until evenly golden brown on all sides, about 12 to 14 minutes. 7. In a large serving bowl, combine the cooled roasted squash and shallots, the toasted bread pieces, and the sliced kale, pomegranate seeds, and chopped celery. Drizzle the dressing over top and toss evenly to combine. Let the salad sit for 5 to 10 minutes before serving, so that some of the dressing can permeate the crisp pieces of bread. Roughly chop the celery leaves to garnish the top of the salad. Serve immediately.

Per Serving

Calories: 333 | fat: 13g | protein: 12g | carbs: 43g | fiber: 8g

Rice Salad with Fennel, Orange and Chickpeas

Prep time: 15 minutes | Cook time: 50 minutes | Serves 4

1½ cups brown basmati rice
1 fennel bulb, trimmed and diced
1 orange, zested, peeled, and segmented (zest and segments reserved)
¼ cup finely chopped parsley
2 cups cooked chickpeas, or 1 (15-ounce / 425-g) can, drained and rinsed
¼ cup plus 2 tablespoons white wine vinegar
½ teaspoon crushed red pepper flakes

1. Rinse the rice under cold water and drain. Add it to a pot with 3 cups of cold water. Bring it to a boil over high heat, reduce the heat to medium, and cook, covered, for 45 to 50 minutes, or until the rice is tender. 2. While the rice cooks, combine the chickpeas, fennel, orange zest and segments, white wine vinegar, crushed red pepper flakes, and parsley in a large bowl and mix well. When the rice is finished, add the rice to the bowl and mix well.

Per Serving

Calories: 317 | fat: 11g | protein: 14g | carbs: 54g | fiber: 18g

Warm Sweet Potato and Brussels Sprout Salad

Prep time: 20 minutes | Cook time: 30 minutes | Serves 4

3 sweet potatoes, peeled and cut into ¼-inch dice
1 teaspoon garlic powder
1 pound (454 g) Brussels sprouts
¼ cup reduced-sugar dried cranberries
Freshly ground black pepper, to taste
1 teaspoon dried thyme
½ teaspoon onion powder
1 cup walnuts, chopped
2 tablespoons balsamic vinegar

1. Preheat the oven to 450°F (235°C). Line a baking sheet with parchment paper. 2. Place the sweet potatoes in a colander and rinse. Shake the colander to remove excess water. Sprinkle the damp sweet potatoes with the thyme, garlic powder, and onion powder. Toss to coat evenly with the spices. Transfer to the prepared baking sheet and spread the sweet potatoes in a single layer. 3. Bake for 20 minutes. Flip the sweet potatoes and bake for 10 minutes more, until fork-tender. 4. While the sweet potatoes roast, wash the Brussels sprouts and remove any tough or discolored outer leaves. Using a large chef's knife, halve the Brussels lengthwise. Place them cut-side down and thinly slice the sprouts crosswise into thin shreds. Discard the root end and loosen the shreds. 5. In a large bowl, toss together the Brussels sprouts, sweet potatoes, walnuts, and cranberries. Drizzle with the vinegar and season with pepper.

Per Serving

Calories: 360 | fat: 20g | protein: 10g | carbs: 44g | fiber: 12g

Mango Black Bean Salad

Prep time: 25 minutes | Cook time: 0 minutes | Serves 4

4 cups cooked black beans, or 2 (15-ounce / 425-g) cans, drained and rinsed
1 bunch green onions (green and white parts), thinly sliced
½ cup red wine vinegar
Zest and juice of 1 orange
2 mangoes, peeled, halved, pitted, and diced
1 medium red bell pepper, seeded and diced small
½ cup finely chopped cilantro
1 jalapeño pepper, minced (for less heat, remove the seeds)
Zest and juice of 1 lime

1. Combine all ingredients in a large bowl and mix well. Chill for 1 hour before serving.

Per Serving

Calories: 299 | fat: 1g | protein: 16g | carbs: 56g | fiber: 17g

Bean and Corn Salad

Prep time: 15 minutes | Cook time: 0 minutes | Serves 6

1 (15-ounce / 425-g) can pinto beans, drained and rinsed
1 (15-ounce / 425-g) can chickpeas, drained and rinsed
¾ cup diced tomato
3 to 4 tablespoons lemon or lime juice
1 (15-ounce / 425-g) can black beans, drained and rinsed
1 (15-ounce / 425-g) can unsalted corn, drained and rinsed
¼ cup chopped cilantro
Salt, to taste (optional)

1. In a large bowl, mix together all the ingredients. The salad can be served chilled or at room temperature.

Per Serving

Calories: 200 | fat: 30g | protein: 10g | carbs: 38g | fiber: 9g

Mexican-Inspired Salad and Sweet Vinaigrette

Prep time: 10 minutes | Cook time: 0 minutes | Serves 4

Salad:

3 cups chopped spinach
⅓ cup diced red onion
⅓ cup dried cranberries or raisins
½ cup cilantro leaves
⅓ cup chopped raw pecans or walnuts

Dressing:

2 tablespoons balsamic vinegar
1 tablespoon olive oil (optional)
½ to 1 tablespoon maple syrup (optional)

1. In a large bowl, combine the spinach, cilantro, onion, pecans (or walnuts), and dried cranberries (or raisins). 2. In a separate small bowl, whisk together the balsamic vinegar, maple syrup, and olive oil, if desired. 3. Pour the dressing over the salad and toss together to thoroughly coat.

Per Serving

Calories: 126 | fat: 8g | protein: 2g | carbs: 11g | fiber: 2g

White Beans Summer Salad

Prep time: 10 minutes | Cook time: 0 minutes | Serves 2

2 cups cooked or canned white beans
8 sun-dried tomatoes, minced
1 tablespoon fresh or dried thyme
½ cubed cucumber
4 tangerines

Optional Toppings:

Black pepper
Tahini

1. When using dry white beans, soak and cook ⅔ cup of dry white beans if necessary. 2. Transfer the white beans to a large bowl, and add the minced sun-dried tomatoes, cucumber cubes and thyme. If using fresh thyme, chop it finely before adding it to the bowl. 3. Stir thoroughly using a spatula and make sure everything is mixed evenly. 4. Peel and section the tangerines and set them aside to garnish the salad. 5. Divide the white beans salad between two bowls, garnish with the tangerine and the optional toppings, serve and enjoy! 6. Store the salad in an airtight container in the fridge, and consume within 2 days. Alternatively, store in the freezer for a maximum of 30 days and thaw at room temperature. The salad can be served cold.

Per Serving

Calories: 376 | fat: 2g | protein: 22g | carbs: 68g | fiber: 17g

Larb Salad

Prep time: 15 minutes | Cook time: 5 minutes | Serves 4

1 teaspoon canola oil (optional)
1 (14-ounce / 397-g) block extra-firm tofu, pressed and crumbled
3 tablespoons lime juice, divided
2½ tablespoons minced cilantro
2 tablespoons soy sauce
1 green onion, sliced
½ tablespoon minced jalapeño
¼ cup thinly sliced red, white, or yellow onion
2 tablespoons minced mint
8 iceberg or romaine lettuce leaves

1. Heat the oil (if desired) in a saucepan over medium heat. Add the tofu and 1 tablespoon of the lime juice, and sauté for 4 to 5 minutes or until the tofu is light brown. 2. Place the tofu in a medium bowl and combine with the remaining 2 tablespoons lime juice, cilantro, soy sauce, green onion, jalapeño, onion, and mint. Mix well. 3. Serve in the lettuce leaves.

Per Serving

Calories: 245 | fat: 10g | protein: 18g | carbs: 26g | fiber: 9g

Southwestern Black Bean Pasta Salad

Prep time: 15 minutes | Cook time: 15 minutes | Serves 4

8 ounces (227 g) whole wheat rotini pasta
2 tablespoons freshly squeezed lime juice
1 teaspoon smoked paprika
1 garlic clove, chopped
1 (15-ounce /425-g) black beans, drained and rinsed
1 pint cherry tomatoes, halved
½ cup chopped fresh cilantro
1 large avocado, halved and pitted
1½ teaspoons chili powder
1 teaspoon ground cumin
1 (15-ounce /425-g) can corn, drained
1 small red bell pepper, diced
¼ cup chopped red onion

1. Cook the pasta according to package instructions. Drain, rinse lightly, and let cool. 2. Scoop the avocado flesh into a blender and add the lime juice, chili powder, paprika, cumin, and garlic. Blend until smooth. 3. In a large bowl, toss together the pasta, corn, black beans, bell pepper, tomatoes, red onion, cilantro, and dressing until well mixed. Refrigerate for at least 1 hour before serving or, for best results, up to 1 day.

Per Serving

Calories: 478 | fat: 10g | protein: 18g | carbs: 84g | fiber: 17g

Chapter 7 Beans and Grains

Vegetable Biryani

Prep time: 30 minutes | Cook time: 1 hour 10 minutes | Serves 4 to 6

Rice:

2 cups brown basmati rice
1 teaspoon ground cumin
½ teaspoon ground cardamom
Salt, to taste (optional)
2 teaspoons turmeric
1 teaspoon ground coriander
½ teaspoon ground cinnamon

Vegetables:

1 medium yellow onion, peeled and diced
1 small head cauliflower, cut into florets (about 3 cups)
6 cloves garlic, peeled and minced
1 teaspoon whole cumin seeds, toasted and ground
½ cup golden raisins
Salt, to taste (optional)
2 stalks broccoli, cut into florets
2 medium carrots, peeled and thinly sliced
2 teaspoons ground coriander
2 tablespoons grated ginger
¼ cup sliced almonds, toasted

Make the Rice: 1. Bring 4 cups of water to a boil in a medium saucepan. Add the rice and bring the pot back to a boil over high heat. Reduce the heat to medium and cook the rice, covered, for 40 minutes. Stir in the turmeric, cumin, coriander, cardamom, and cinnamon, season with salt (if using), and cook for another 5 minutes, or until the rice is tender. Make the Vegetables: 2. Place the onion in a large saucepan and sauté over medium heat for 8 minutes. Add water 1 to 2 tablespoons at a time to keep the onion from sticking to the pan. Add the broccoli, cauliflower, and carrots to the pan and cook until the vegetables are tender, 8 to 10 minutes. Add the garlic, coriander, cumin, and ginger, mix well, and cook for another 5 minutes. Add the cooked rice, raisins, and almonds. Season with additional salt (if using) and mix well.

Per Serving

Calories: 339 | fat: 4g | protein: 8g | carbs: 68g | fiber: 5g

Orange Quinoa with Black Beans

Prep time: 15 minutes | Cook time: 20 minutes | Serves 4

1½ cups quinoa, rinsed and drained
2 cups cooked black beans, or 1 (15-ounce / 425-g) can, drained and rinsed
Zest and juice of 1 orange (about ¼ cup juice)
Salt and freshly ground black pepper, to taste
1½ teaspoons cumin seeds, toasted and ground
1½ teaspoons grated ginger
2 tablespoons balsamic vinegar
4 green onions (white and green parts), thinly sliced

1. Add 3 cups of water to a medium pot with a tight-fitting lid and bring to a boil over high heat. Add the quinoa and return the pot to a boil over high heat. Reduce the heat to medium-low and cook the quinoa, covered, for 15 to 20 minutes, or until tender. 2. Place the quinoa in a large bowl and add the cumin, black beans, ginger, vinegar, orange zest and juice, and green onions. Mix well and season with salt and pepper.

Per Serving

Calories: 369 | fat: 4g | protein: 16g | carbs: 65g | fiber: 12g

Thai-Inspired Rice Bowl

Prep time: 30 minutes | Cook time: 45 minutes | Serves 4

Peanut Sauce:

3 tablespoons creamy peanut butter
1 tablespoon packed lime zest
1 tablespoon grated peeled fresh ginger
½ teaspoon red pepper flakes
2 tablespoons freshly squeezed lime juice
1 tablespoon coconut aminos
2 garlic cloves, minced

Rice Bowl:

1½ cups water
1 small red cabbage, shredded
1 yellow bell pepper, cut into slices
1 shallot, cut into slices
¼ cup fresh cilantro, chopped
Juice of 1 lime
¾ cup brown rice
1 red bell pepper, cut into slices
1 cup shelled edamame
1 carrot, cut into matchsticks
1 bunch chopped scallions, green parts only

Make the Peanut Sauce: 1. In a medium bowl, whisk together the peanut butter, lime juice and zest, coconut aminos, ginger, garlic, and red pepper flakes to combine. Set aside. Make the Rice Bowl: 2. In a medium pot over high heat, bring the water to a boil. Stir in the brown rice. Bring to a simmer, reduce the heat to medium-low, cover the pot, and cook, undisturbed, for 35 to 40 minutes. Check the rice after 35 minutes to see if the water has been absorbed. Remove from the heat. 3. In a large bowl, toss together the brown rice, red cabbage, red and yellow bell peppers, edamame, shallot, carrot, cilantro, scallions, and lime juice. Serve with a drizzle of peanut sauce.

Per Serving

Calories: 323 | fat: 9g | protein: 14g | carbs: 54g | fiber: 11g

BLAT (Bacon, Lettuce, Avocado and Tomato) Pitas

Prep time: 10 minutes | Cook time: 5 minutes | Makes 4 sandwiches

2 teaspoons coconut oil (optional)
Few drops liquid smoke
2 avocados, sliced
2 sliced scallions
4 8-inch whole wheat pitas
4 sliced plum tomatoes
½ cup dulse, picked through and separated
Salt and black pepper (optional)
¼ cup chopped cilantro
2 tablespoons lime juice
4 cups greens

1. Place a large cast-iron skillet over medium heat. Once it's warm, add the coconut oil (if desired), then the dulse and liquid smoke. Toss to combine. Cook, stirring often, until the dulse is crispy, about 5 minutes. Remove from the heat and season with pepper to taste. 2. Mash the avocado with the cilantro, scallions, and lime juice. Season with salt and pepper to taste, if desired. 3. Slice the pitas in half and toast lightly. Gently open them, and divide the avocado mixture evenly into all 8 halves. Divide the greens, tomatoes, and dulse evenly among the pitas and serve.

Per Serving (1 sandwich)

Calories: 381 | fat: 19g | protein: 10g | carbs: 50g | fiber: 14g

Ras El Hanout Protein Bowl

Prep time: 15 minutes | Cook time: 35 minutes | Serves 3

1 cup cooked or canned chickpeas
⅔ cup dry green lentils
2 tablespoons Ras el Hanout
¼ cup dry quinoa
3 cups vegetable stock

Optional Toppings:
Raisins
Tahini
Parsley

1. When using dry chickpeas, soak and cook ⅓ cup of dry chickpeas. 2. Put a large pot over medium-high heat and add the vegetable stock and the lentils to the pot. 3. Bring the water to a boil, then turn the heat down to medium. 4. Cook the lentils for about 15 minutes without covering the pot. Stir occasionally and remove any foam produced by the lentils. 5. Add the quinoa and Ras el Hanout spices, then cook for another 15 minutes, stirring occasionally. 6. Add the chickpeas and stir well, then bring the heat down to a simmer and leave to simmer for about 5 minutes. 7. Turn the heat off and let the mixture cool down for a minute. 8. Divide between 2 bowls, garnish with the optional toppings, serve and enjoy! 9. Store in an airtight container in the fridge, and consume within 2 days. Alternatively, store in the freezer, for a maximum of 30 days and thaw at room temperature. The bowl can be served cold or reheated in a saucepan or a microwave.

Per Serving
Calories: 353 | fat: 5g | protein: 20g | carbs: 56g | fiber: 20g

Hearty Chickpea Burgers

Prep time: 15 minutes | Cook time: 10 minutes | Serves 4

2 tablespoons ground flaxseed
1 cup raw walnuts
1 garlic clove, peeled and stemmed
1 teaspoon chili powder
½ teaspoon garlic powder
¾ cup canned chickpeas, drained and rinsed
1 tablespoon apple cider vinegar
¼ cup water
½ cup whole wheat bread crumbs or gluten-free bread crumbs
1 teaspoon smoked paprika
¼ teaspoon onion powder
3 tablespoons peanut butter

1. In a small bowl, whisk together the flaxseed and water. Set aside. 2. In a food processor, combine the walnuts, bread crumbs, garlic, chili powder, paprika, garlic powder, and onion powder. Process for about 2 minutes until crumbly. Add the soaked flaxseed, the chickpeas, peanut butter, and vinegar. Process for 1 to 2 minutes, or until fully combined. 3. Transfer the mixture to a large bowl and knead for 1 to 2 minutes, or until the mixture comes together and can be shaped. Divide the dough into 4 equal parts and shape into ½-inch-thick patties. 4. In a nonstick skillet over medium heat, cook the patties for 3 to 5 minutes per side until browned and crispy. Serve immediately.

Per Serving
Calories: 338 | fat: 25g | protein: 11g | carbs: 22g | fiber: 7g

Black and White Bean Chili

Prep time: 10 minutes | Cook time: 20 minutes | Serves 4

1 teaspoon extra-virgin olive oil (optional)
1 large carrot, peeled and diced small
1 small zucchini, diced small
1 (15-ounce / 425-g) can black beans, drained and rinsed
1 cup frozen corn
½ teaspoon salt (optional)
½ teaspoon garlic powder
2 tablespoons minced fresh cilantro, for garnish
1 scallion, white and green parts, thinly sliced, for garnish
1 avocado, peeled, pitted, and diced, for garnish
½ yellow onion, diced small
1 red or yellow bell pepper, seeded and diced small
1 (15-ounce / 425-g) can cannellini beans, drained and rinsed
1 (28-ounce / 794-g) can crushed tomatoes
1 teaspoon chili powder
½ teaspoon ground cumin
1 cup water
Pinch red pepper flakes, for garnish
1 jalapeño pepper, cut into slices, for garnish (optional)
1 lime, cut into wedges, for garnish

1. In a large pot, heat the olive oil over medium heat. Add the onion, carrot, bell pepper, and zucchini and cook, stirring often, until fragrant and the vegetables start to get tender, about 10 minutes. 2. Raise the heat to medium-high, add the cannellini beans, black beans, tomatoes, corn, chili powder, salt (if using), cumin, garlic powder, and water, stir well, and bring to a boil. Lower the heat to medium-low and simmer until heated through and the flavors meld, about 5 more minutes. 3. Spoon the chili into bowls and garnish with cilantro, red pepper flakes, scallion, jalapeño (if using), avocado, and a lime wedge.

Per Serving

Calories: 329 | fat: 3g | protein: 17g | carbs: 65g | fiber: 20g

Berbere-Spiced Red Lentils

Prep time: 5 minutes | Cook time: 25 minutes | Serves 4

1 cup dried red lentils, rinsed
1 teaspoon extra-virgin olive oil (optional)
½ medium yellow onion, chopped small
2 tablespoons Berbere spice
2 teaspoons tomato paste
3 cups water
2 garlic cloves, minced
3 tomatoes, chopped
1 teaspoon salt (optional)

1. In a large saucepan, combine the lentils and water over high heat and bring to a boil. Lower the heat to medium-low and cook, checking occasionally and adding more water if needed, for 20 minutes. 2. In a medium skillet, heat the olive oil over medium heat. Add the garlic and onion and cook until fragrant, 3 to 5 minutes 3. Add the tomatoes, Berbere spice, salt (if using), and tomato paste and cook, stirring constantly, until the mixture turns a deep red and becomes paste-like, about 5 minutes. Set aside. 4. Add the spiced tomato-and-onion mixture to the lentils and simmer over medium heat until the flavors combine and it's very thick, about 5 minutes. Serve immediately.

Per Serving

Calories: 216 | fat: 3g | protein: 13g | carbs: 38g | fiber: 8g

Chana Masala

Prep time: 10 minutes | Cook time: 25 minutes | Serves 2

2 cups cooked or canned chickpeas
2 medium onions, minced
¼ cup water
1 cup canned or fresh tomato cubes
2 tablespoons curry spices

Optional Toppings:

Fresh chili slices
Shredded coconut
Lime juice

1. When using dry chickpeas, soak and cook ⅔ cup of dry chickpeas. 2. Put a large pot over medium heat, then add the tomato cubes, onions, and the water. 3. Cook for a few minutes, stirring occasionally, until everything is cooked, then add the curry spices and stir thoroughly. 4. Add the chickpeas, and stir thoroughly to make sure that everything is well mixed. 5. Cook for a couple more minutes, stirring occasionally, then lower the heat to a simmer. 6. Let the curry simmer for about 20 minutes while stirring occasionally. 7. Turn the heat off and let the curry cool down for a minute. 8. Divide curry between 2 bowls, garnish with the optional toppings, serve and enjoy! 9. Store the curry in an airtight container in the fridge, and consume within 2 days. Alternatively, store in the freezer for a maximum of 30 days and thaw at room temperature. Reheat the curry in the microwave or a saucepan.

Per Serving

Calories: 401 | fat: 6g | protein: 21g | carbs: 64g | fiber: 20g

Mushroom Barley Risotto

Prep time: 20 minutes | Cook time: 55 minutes | Serves 3 to 4

1 ounce (28 g) dried porcini mushrooms, soaked for 30 minutes in 1 cup of water that has just been boiled
2 sage leaves, minced
1½ cups pearled barley
3 to 4 cups vegetable stock, or low-sodium vegetable broth
3 large shallots, peeled and finely diced
8 ounces (227 g) cremini mushrooms, sliced
3 cloves garlic, peeled and minced
½ cup dry white wine
¼ cup nutritional yeast (optional)
Salt and freshly ground black pepper, to taste

1. Drain the porcini mushrooms, reserving the liquid. Finely chop the mushrooms and set aside. 2. Place the shallots in a 2-quart saucepan and sauté over medium heat for 4 to 5 minutes. Add water 1 to 2 tablespoons at a time to keep the shallots from sticking to the pan. Add the cremini mushrooms and cook for another 5 minutes. Let the mushrooms brown by adding as little water as possible, while still making sure they don't stick to the pan. Add the sage, garlic, barley, and white wine and cook for 1 minute. Add 2 cups of the vegetable stock and the 1 cup of reserved porcini soaking liquid and bring the mixture to a boil over high heat. 3. Reduce the heat to medium and cook, covered, for 25 minutes. Add more broth if necessary and cook for another 15 to 20 minutes. Stir in the chopped porcini mushrooms and nutritional yeast (if using). Season with salt and pepper and serve immediately.

Per Serving

Calories: 354 | fat: 2g | protein: 15g | carbs: 74g | fiber: 16g

Almost Instant Ramen

Prep time: 15 minutes | Cook time: 15 minutes | Serves 6

6 cups vegetable broth
2 tablespoons wakame (optional)
1 teaspoon toasted sesame seeds
¼ teaspoon crushed red pepper, or more to taste
2 cups shredded red cabbage
½ cup kimchi
2 (3 ounces / 85 g) packages gluten-free ramen or soba noodles
2 scallions, sliced thin
1 small yellow onion, diced
1 teaspoon minced or grated fresh ginger, or more to taste
2 cups broccoli florets
2 carrots, finely chopped
8 ounces (227 g) extra-firm tofu, cubed
2 tablespoons gluten-free red miso, or more to taste
2 nori sheets, cut into strips (optional)
Chopped cilantro

1. Bring the broth to a boil in a large stockpot. Add the onion, wakame (if desired), ginger, sesame seeds, and crushed red pepper. 2. Reduce the heat to medium and add the broccoli, cabbage, carrots, kimchi, and tofu. Cook for 3 minutes. 3. Add the noodles, increase the heat to medium-high, and cook for 5 minutes or according to the package instructions. 4. Remove from the heat. Whisk in the miso and serve with the nori, scallions, and cilantro.

Per Serving

Calories: 135 | fat: 3g | protein: 8g | carbs: 22g | fiber: 2g

Eggplant and Chickpea Rice Pilaf

Prep time: 20 minutes | Cook time: 1 hour 10 minutes | Serves 4

2 cups vegetable stock, or low-sodium vegetable broth
6 cloves garlic, peeled and minced
1 tablespoon cumin seeds, toasted and ground
1 teaspoon turmeric
2 cups cooked chickpeas, or 1 (15-ounce / 425-g) can, drained and rinsed
½ cup finely chopped basil
½ cup finely chopped cilantro
1 cup brown basmati rice
1 large yellow onion, peeled and diced small
2 jalapeño peppers, seeded and minced
1 tablespoon ground coriander
1 large eggplant, stemmed and cut into ½-inch cubes
¼ cup finely chopped mint
Salt, to taste (optional)

1. Bring the vegetable stock to a boil in a medium saucepan. Add the rice and bring the mixture back to a boil over high heat. Reduce the heat to medium and cook, covered, until the rice is tender, about 45 minutes. 2. Place the onion in a large saucepan and sauté over medium heat for 7 to 8 minutes. Add water 1 to 2 tablespoons at a time to keep the onion from sticking to the pan. Add the garlic, jalapeño peppers, cumin, coriander, turmeric, and eggplant and cook until the eggplant is tender, about 12 minutes. Add the cooked rice, chickpeas, mint, and basil. Season with salt (if using) and serve garnished with the cilantro.

Per Serving

Calories: 373 | fat: 4g | protein: 13g | carbs: 73g | fiber: 12g

Basic Polenta

Prep time: 2 minutes | Cook time: 30 minutes | Serves 4 to 6

1½ cups coarse cornmeal
¾ teaspoon salt, or to taste (optional)

Bring 5 cups of water to a boil in a large saucepan. Whisk in the cornmeal, a little at a time. Cook, stirring often, until the mixture is thick and creamy, about 30 minutes. Season with salt (if using) and serve, or pour the polenta into a pan and refrigerate until set, about 1 hour.

Per Serving

Calories: 145 | fat: 0g | protein: 2g | carbs: 31g | fiber: 1g

White Beans and Escarole with Parsnips

Prep time: 20 minutes | Cook time: 30 minutes | Serves 4

1 medium yellow onion, peeled and diced
4 cloves garlic, peeled and minced
4 cups cooked cannellini beans, or 2 (15-ounce / 425-g) cans, drained and rinsed
2 large parsnips, peeled and diced
1 large head escarole, soaked in cool water, rinsed well to remove any dirt, and chopped
Salt and freshly ground black pepper, to taste

1. Place the onion in a large skillet and sauté over medium heat for 5 minutes. Add water 1 to 2 tablespoons at a time to keep the onion from sticking to the pan. 2. Add the parsnips and garlic and cook for 4 minutes. Add the escarole and cook until tender, about 15 minutes. Add the beans, season with salt and pepper, and cook for 5 minutes longer.

Per Serving

Calories: 127 | fat: 1g | protein: 4g | carbs: 28g | fiber: 9g

Spicy Chickpeas and Fennel

Prep time: 15 minutes | Cook time: 35 minutes | Serves 4

1 large yellow onion, peeled and chopped
4 cloves garlic, peeled and minced
1½ teaspoons ground fennel seeds
1 (28-ounce / 794-g) can diced tomatoes
Chopped flat-leaf Italian parsley
1 large fennel bulb, trimmed and thinly sliced
1 tablespoon minced oregano
1 teaspoon crushed red pepper flakes
4 cups cooked chickpeas, or 2 (15-ounce / 425-g) cans, drained and rinsed

1. Place the onion and fennel in a large saucepan, and sauté over medium heat for 10 minutes, or until the vegetables are tender. Add water 1 to 2 tablespoons at a time to keep the vegetables from sticking to the pan. 2. Add the garlic, oregano, fennel seeds, and crushed red pepper flakes and cook for 3 minutes. Add the tomatoes and chickpeas and bring the pan to a boil over high heat. Reduce the heat to medium and cook, covered, for 20 minutes. Serve garnished with the parsley.

Per Serving

Calories: 343 | fat: 5g | protein: 17g | carbs: 61g | fiber: 19g

Sweet Potato and Cauliflower Rice Pilaf

Prep time: 30 minutes | Cook time: 1 hour 25 minutes | Serves 4

3 to 3½ cups vegetable stock, or low-sodium vegetable broth
2 whole cloves
1 medium yellow onion, peeled and cut into ½-inch dice
½ small head cauliflower, cut into florets
2 cloves garlic, peeled and minced
½ cup chopped cilantro
Salt, to taste (optional)
1½ cups brown basmati rice
1 large cinnamon stick
2 cardamom pods
1 medium carrot, peeled and cut into ½-inch dice
1 medium sweet potato, peeled and cut into ½-inch dice
1 cup peas, thawed if frozen
1 large pinch saffron, soaked in 3 tablespoons hot water

1. Bring 3 cups of the vegetable stock to a boil and add the rice, cinnamon stick, cloves, and cardamom pods. Bring the mixture back to a boil over high heat, then reduce the heat to medium and cook, covered, until the rice is tender, about 45 minutes. Check the rice for tenderness and add more stock, if needed, and cook for another 10 minutes if necessary. Remove the cinnamon stick, cloves, and cardamom pods before serving. 2. Place the onion in a large saucepan and sauté over medium-high heat for 7 to 8 minutes, or until the onion is tender and starting to brown. Add water 1 to 2 tablespoons at a time to keep the onion from sticking to the pan. Add the carrot and sweet potato and cook for 10 minutes. Add the cauliflower and garlic and cook 6 to 7 minutes longer, or until the cauliflower is tender. Add the peas, cilantro, and saffron and its soaking liquid and season with salt (if using). Add the cooked rice and mix well.

Per Serving

Calories: 352 | fat: 2g | protein: 9g | carbs: 64g | fiber: 7g

Mac 'N' Mince

Prep time: 15 minutes | Cook time: 10 minutes | Serves 4

2 cups whole wheat macaroni
½ cup tahini
2 tablespoons lemon garlic pepper seasoning
2 tablespoons turmeric (optional)
1 (7-ounce / 198-g) pack textured soy mince
¼ cup nutritional yeast
½ cup water

Optional Toppings:

Sun-dried tomatoes
Crispy onions

1. Cook the macaroni and set it aside afterwards. 2. Put a nonstick deep frying pan over medium high heat and add the soy mince with the ¼ cup of water. 3. Stir fry the soy mince until it is cooked and most of the water has evaporated. 4. Add the tahini, ¼ cup of water, nutritional yeast, lemon garlic pepper seasoning and the optional turmeric to the soy mince. 5. Cook a little longer, stirring continuously, until everything is well combined. 6. Add the cooked macaroni to the pan with soy mince and stir thoroughly until the mac 'N' mince is mixed well. 7. Divide the mac 'N' mince between two plates, serve with the optional toppings and enjoy! 8. Store the mac 'N' mince in an airtight container in the fridge, and consume within 3 days. Alternatively, store it in the freezer for a maximum of 30 days and thaw at room temperature. Use a microwave, toaster oven, or frying pan to reheat the mac 'n' mince.

Per Serving

Calories: 454 | fat: 20g | protein: 25g | carbs: 42g | fiber: 10g

Barley Bowl with Cranberries and Walnuts

Prep time: 5 minutes | Cook time: 30 minutes | Serves 4

1 cup pearl barley, uncooked
¼ cup poppy seeds
½ cup chopped walnuts, toasted
3 cups water
½ cup dried cranberries

1. In a medium pot, combine the barley and water and bring to a boil. Reduce the heat to medium and cook until the barley is tender, 25 to 30 minutes. Once done, drain off any excess water and let cool. 2. While the barley is cooking, place the poppy seeds and dried cranberries in a small bowl and soak them in hot water for 5 to 10 minutes; then drain the water and let cool. 3. In a large bowl, combine the cooked barley, cranberries, poppy seeds, and walnuts. Mix well, cover, and refrigerate for 30 minutes to 1 hour before serving cold.

Per Serving

Calories: 341 | fat: 14g | protein: 9g | carbs: 50g | fiber: 11g

Fried Rice with Tofu Scramble

Prep time: 15 minutes | Cook time: 35 minutes | Serves 2

4 cups cooked quick-cooking brown rice
1 (7-ounce / 198-g) pack extra-firm tofu, scrambled
¼ cup curry spices
1 cup cooked or canned green peas
1 cup julienned carrots
1 cup water

Optional Toppings:

Lemon slices
Fresh cilantro
Sauerkraut

1. Cook 1½ cup of brown rice for about 25 minutes. 2. Put a large nonstick frying pan over medium heat and add ½ cup of water and the tofu scramble. 3. Add the curry spices and cook for about 5 minutes, stirring occasionally to prevent the tofu from sticking to the pan, until the tofu is well heated and most of the water has evaporated. 4. Add the carrots, rice, and green peas along with the remaining ½ cup water and stir-fry for another 5 minutes or until the water has evaporated. 5. Turn off the heat, divide the fried rice between 2 bowls, serve with the optional toppings and enjoy! 6. Store the fried rice in an airtight container in the fridge, and consume within 3 days. Alternatively, store in the freezer for a maximum of 30 days and thaw at room temperature. Reheat the fried rice in a nonstick frying pan or microwave.

Per Serving

Calories: 286 | fat: 10g | protein: 18g | carbs: 30g | fiber: 8g

Smoky Cajun Bowl

Prep time: 20 minutes | Cook time: 25 minutes | Serves 4

2 cups cooked or canned black beans
1 (7-ounce / 198-g) pack smoked tofu, cubed
1 tablespoon salt-free Cajun spices
1 cup dry quick-cooking brown rice
2 cups canned or fresh tomato cubes
¼ cup water (optional)

Optional Toppings:

peeled slices
Avocado slices
Fresh cilantro

1. When using dry beans, soak and cook ⅔ cup of dry black beans if necessary. And cook the brown rice. 2. Put a nonstick deep frying pan over medium-high heat and add the tofu cubes, tomato cubes and the optional ¼ cup of water. 3. Stir occasionally until everything is cooked, then add the black beans, cooked brown rice and Cajun spices. 4. Turn the heat off and stir occasionally for about 5 minutes until everything is heated through. 5. Divide the smoky Cajun beans and rice between 4 bowls, serve with the optional toppings and enjoy! 6. Store the smoky Cajun beans and rice in an airtight container in the fridge, and consume within 3 days. Alternatively, store in the freezer for a maximum of 30 days and thaw at room temperature. Use a microwave, toaster oven, or nonstick frying pan to reheat the smoky Cajun beans and rice.

Per Serving

Calories: 371 | fat: 5g | protein: 20g | carbs: 60g | fiber: 12g

Chapter 8 Desserts

Stone Fruit Compote

Prep time: 5 minutes | Cook time: 10 minutes | Makes 2½ cups

1½ pounds (680 g) ripe peaches, plums, apricots, or cherries
Tiny pinch of fine sea salt (optional)
2 teaspoons filtered water
½ cup freshly squeezed orange juice or filtered water
1 teaspoon arrowroot powder
½ teaspoon vanilla extract

1. If using peaches, plums, or apricots, halve and pit them. Cut each half into ½-inch wedges and slice the wedges in half crosswise. If using cherries, pit them. Put the fruit in a medium pot, add the orange juice and salt, and bring to a simmer over high heat. Cover the pot, reduce the heat to low, and simmer for 8 to 10 minutes, until the fruit is soft. Dissolve the arrowroot in the water in a small cup, then drizzle it into the pot, stirring constantly. Once the compote has returned to a simmer and thickened, remove from the heat and stir in the vanilla. 2. Serve warm or at room temperature. Store the cooled compote in a sealed jar in the fridge for up to 5 days.

Per Serving (½ cup)

Calories: 77 | fat: 0g | protein: 1g | carbs: 19g | fiber: 2g

Vanilla Corn Cake with Roasted Strawberries

Prep time: 20 minutes | Cook time: 50 minutes | Makes 1 cake

¾ cup full-fat coconut milk
1 cup cornmeal
1 teaspoon lemon zest
¼ teaspoon baking soda
½ teaspoon ground turmeric (optional)
½ cup coconut oil, plus extra to grease pan
1 teaspoon vanilla bean paste or pure vanilla extract
1 teaspoon fresh lemon juice
1 cup whole spelt flour
1 tablespoon aluminum-free baking powder
1 teaspoon fine sea salt (optional)
½ cup plus 2 tablespoons pure maple syrup (optional)
4 cups whole strawberries

1. Preheat the oven to 350°F (180°C). Lightly grease a 9-inch round cake pan with coconut oil. Cut a circle of parchment paper to fit in the bottom of the pan and press it in. Lightly grease the parchment, and set aside. 2. In a medium bowl, whisk together the coconut milk and lemon juice. Let this mixture sit for 5 minutes so that the milk can curdle slightly. 3. In a large bowl, whisk together the cornmeal, spelt flour, lemon zest, baking powder, baking soda, sea salt, and turmeric, if using. 4. Make a well in the center of the cornmeal mixture. Add the maple syrup, oil, if using, vanilla, and coconut milk mixture. With a spatula, gently mix until you have a smooth and unified batter. Avoid overmixing. 5. Scrape the batter into the prepared cake pan and slide the pan into the oven. Bake the cake for 25 to 28 minutes or until the top is golden and a toothpick inserted into the center comes out clean. Let the cake cool completely. Raise the oven temperature to 400°F (205°C). 6. Cut the strawberries into halves or quarters (depending on size), and place them on a parchment-lined baking sheet. Slide the baking sheet into the oven and roast the strawberries until they become juicy and jammy, about 20 minutes. 7. Serve slices of the corn cake with a few roasted strawberries.

Per Serving (⅛ cake)

Calories: 394 | fat: 20g | protein: 6g | carbs: 52g | fiber: 5g

Pumpkin Bread Pudding

Prep time: 10 minutes | Cook time: 25 minutes | Serves 8

1¼ cups pumpkin purée (a little over ½ of a 15-ounce / 425-g can)
½ cup 100% maple syrup (optional)
2 tablespoons cornstarch
½ teaspoon ground cinnamon
¼ teaspoon ground nutmeg
⅛ teaspoon ground cloves
½ cup golden raisins
1 cup unsweetened plant-based milk
1 cup unsweetened plant-based milk
2 teaspoons pure vanilla extract
½ teaspoon salt (optional)
¾ teaspoon ground ginger
¼ teaspoon ground allspice
8 slices stale whole wheat bread, cut into 1-inch cubes (about 6 cups)

1. Preheat the oven to 350°F (180°C). Have ready an 8 × 8-inch nonstick or silicone baking pan. 2. In a large bowl, whisk together the pumpkin purée, plant-based milk, maple syrup (if using), and vanilla. Add the cornstarch, salt (if using), cinnamon, ginger, nutmeg, allspice, and cloves and whisk well. Stir in the bread cubes and raisins, and toss to coat completely. 3. Transfer the mixture to the prepared pan. Bake for 25 minutes, or until the top is golden brown and firm to the touch. Serve warm.

Per Serving

Calories: 192 | fat: 1g | protein: 4g | carbs: 31g | fiber: 2g

Berry Chia Pudding

Prep time: 5 minutes | Cook time: 5 minutes | Makes 3 cups

4 cups fresh or frozen berries
Pinch of fine sea salt (optional)
2 tablespoons coconut butter
6 tablespoons chia seeds
1½ cups freshly squeezed orange juice
½ cup raw cashews or macadamia nuts
2 teaspoons vanilla extract

1. Combine the berries, orange juice, and salt, if using, in a medium pot and bring to a boil over high heat. Cover, reduce the heat to low, and simmer for 5 minutes, or until the berries have softened and released their juices. Remove from the heat and allow to cool slightly. 2. Transfer the mixture to an upright blender, add the cashews, coconut butter, and vanilla, and blend until completely smooth. Pour into a widemouthed quart jar or a medium bowl, add the chia seeds, and whisk thoroughly, making sure there are no clumps of seeds hiding anywhere. Allow to sit for a few minutes and then whisk again. Leave the whisk in place and refrigerate for at least 1 hour, or until completely chilled, whisking every now and then to distribute the chia seeds evenly and to help cool the pudding quickly. The pudding will thicken further overnight; if it gets too thick, stir in a splash of water or nut milk. Store the pudding in an airtight glass jar or other container in the fridge for up to 5 days.

Per Serving (½ cup)

Calories: 211 | fat: 14g | protein: 2g | carbs: 21g | fiber: 5g

Apple-Oat Crisp

Prep time: 10 minutes | Cook time: 25 minutes | Serves 4 to 6

4 medium Granny Smith apples, cored and cut into ½-inch-thick slices
½ teaspoon ground cinnamon
¼ teaspoon tapioca starch
⅔ cup oat flour
¾ cup pure maple syrup, divided
1 tablespoon lemon juice
⅛ teaspoon ground nutmeg
⅔ cup rolled oats
⅓ cup unsweetened applesauce

1. Preheat the oven to 350°F (180°C). 2. In a medium bowl, mix together the apples, ½ cup of maple syrup, the lemon juice, cinnamon, nutmeg, and tapioca starch until the apples are well coated. 3. Spread the apples out in a single layer in an 8-by-8-inch glass baking dish or a 9-inch pie plate. 4. In a medium bowl, mix together the oats, oat flour, remaining ¼ cup of maple syrup, and the applesauce until well combined. Scoop the oat mixture in dollops onto the apples, and spread gently, trying to cover all the apples. 5. Transfer the baking dish to the oven, and bake for 20 to 25 minutes, or until the oat mixture is golden brown. Remove from the oven.

Per Serving

Calories: 344 | fat: 3g | protein: 5g | carbs: 80g | fiber: 9g

Pumpkin Pie Oatmeal Parfaits

Prep time: 20 minutes | Cook time: 7 hours | Makes 6 parfaits

Nonstick cooking spray (optional)
2 cups steel-cut oats
1 (15-ounce / 425-g) can pumpkin purée
1 teaspoon ground nutmeg, divided
½ teaspoon ground ginger
1½ cups rolled oats
¾ cup chopped pecans (optional)
1 (15-ounce / 425-g) can coconut cream
4 cups water
2 teaspoons ground cinnamon, divided
½ teaspoon ground cloves
½ cup maple syrup, plus 3 to 4 tablespoons more for serving (optional)

1. Coat the inside of the slow cooker with cooking spray (if using) or line it with a slow cooker liner. Place the unopened can of coconut cream into the refrigerator to chill. 2. Add the steel-cut oats, water, pumpkin purée, 1 teaspoon of cinnamon, ½ teaspoon of nutmeg, the cloves, ginger, and maple syrup (if using). Stir to combine. Cover and cook on Low for 7 hours. After cooking, stir well. 3. While the steel-cut oats cook, preheat the oven to 350°F (180°C). On a parchment-lined baking sheet, spread out the rolled oats and pecans (if using) in a single layer and sprinkle with the remaining 1 teaspoon of cinnamon and ½ teaspoon of nutmeg. Bake for 10 minutes. Set the crumble aside to cool and store loosely covered at room temperature until the steel-cut oats are done cooking. 4. Just before serving, pour the cold coconut cream into a medium bowl. Using an electric beater, whip the cream for about 1 minute, until it becomes thick. 5. For each parfait, layer 3 tablespoons of the crumble, about ½ teaspoon of the maple syrup (if using), 2 to 3 tablespoons of the warm pumpkin oatmeal, and about 2 tablespoons of the whipped cream. Continue layering in this order until your glass is full, finishing with the whipped cream on top, a sprinkle of the crumble, and a tiny drizzle more of maple syrup.

Per Serving

Calories: 497 | fat: 18g | protein: 11g | carbs: 76g | fiber: 10g

Sweet Potato Pie Nice Cream

Prep time: 5 minutes | Cook time: 0 minutes | Serves 2

2 medium cooked sweet potatoes
1 tablespoon maple syrup (optional)
½ teaspoon ground cinnamon
½ cup plant-based milk
1 teaspoon vanilla extract

1. Line a baking sheet with parchment paper. 2. Remove the skin from the cooked sweet potatoes, and cut the flesh into 1-inch cubes. Place on the baking sheet in an even layer, then place in the freezer overnight, or for a minimum of 4 hours. 3. In a food processor, combine the frozen sweet potato, milk, maple syrup (if desired), vanilla, and cinnamon. 4. Process on medium speed for 1 to 2 minutes, or until the mixture has been blended into a smooth soft-serve consistency, and serve. (If you notice any sweet potato pieces stuck toward the top and sides of the food processor, you may need to stop and scrape them down with a spatula, then pulse until smooth.)

Per Serving

Calories: 155 | fat: 1g | protein: 2g | carbs: 34g | fiber:5 g

Chocolate Lava Mug Cake

Prep time: 10 minutes | Cook time: 5 minutes | Makes 1 cake

¼ cup almond milk
1 tablespoon sugar (optional)
½ teaspoon vanilla extract
¼ cup whole wheat pastry flour
¼ teaspoon baking powder
1 tablespoon cooked, unsweetened adzuki or black beans, mashed well
2 tablespoons unsweetened cocoa powder
⅛ teaspoon salt (optional)
2 tablespoons mini chocolate chips (optional)

1. Combine the almond milk, beans, sugar, and vanilla in a mug. Stir in the cocoa, flour, salt (if desired), and baking powder until just combined. Drop the chocolate chips in the center. 2 Microwave until the cake is set around the edges but the center is soft, about 90 seconds. Let sit for 5 minutes, then eat!

Per Serving

Calories: 209 | fat: 3g | protein: 7g | carbs: 45g | fiber: 8g

Chocolate-Peppermint Nice Cream

Prep time: 5 minutes | Cook time: 0 minutes | Serves 2

3 frozen ripe bananas, broken into thirds
2 tablespoons cocoa powder
3 tablespoons plant-based milk
⅛ teaspoon peppermint extract

1. In a food processor, combine the bananas, milk, cocoa powder, and peppermint. 2. Process on medium speed for 30 to 60 seconds, or until the bananas have been blended into smooth soft-serve consistency, and serve.

Per Serving

Calories: 173 | fat: 2g | protein: 3g | carbs: 43g | fiber: 6g

Caramelized Banana with Yogurt and Toasted Coconut

Prep time: 5 minutes | Cook time: 5 minutes | Serves 1

1 tablespoon maple syrup (optional)
¼ cup plain unsweetened cashew milk yogurt
Pinch ground cinnamon
1 small banana, cut into ¼-inch-thick slices
1 tablespoon toasted shredded coconut

1. Pour the maple syrup (if using) into a small skillet and heat over medium-low heat. Add the bananas and caramelize for 3 to 5 minutes. 2. Put the yogurt on a small plate or in a small bowl. Place the caramelized bananas on top of the yogurt, and sprinkle with the shredded coconut and cinnamon.

Per Serving

Calories: 196 | fat: 3g | protein: 3g | carbs: 43g | fiber: 3g

Vanilla Bean Whip

Prep time: 5 minutes | Cook time: 0 minutes | Makes 2 cups

1 (12-ounce / 340-g) package extra-firm silken tofu, drained
2 tablespoons fresh lemon juice
1 vanilla bean
½ cup cashews, soaked overnight and drained
½ cup 100% pure maple syrup (optional)
Pinch salt (optional)

1. Combine the tofu, cashews, maple syrup (if using), lemon juice, and salt (if using) in a blender. Purée until smooth. Scrape down the sides of the blender to incorporate all the ingredients. 2. Slice the vanilla bean in half lengthwise with a sharp knife and scrape the seeds into the blender. Blend the mixture until very smooth. 3. Transfer the mixture to a bowl and cover with plastic wrap. Chill for several hours in the refrigerator, or until firm.

Per Serving

Calories: 143 | fat: 6g | protein: 5g | carbs: 17g | fiber: 0g

Protein Chocolate Chip Cookies

Prep time: 10 minutes | Cook time: 20 minutes | Makes 12 cookies

1 teaspoon canola oil, for greasing (optional)
½ cup creamy or chunky peanut butter
1½ teaspoons vanilla extract
⅛ teaspoon salt (optional)
1 (15-ounce / 425-g) can chickpeas, drained and rinsed
¼ teaspoon baking powder
¾ cup vegan semisweet chocolate chips

1. Preheat the oven to 350°F (180°C), and lightly grease a baking sheet. 2. In a food processor or high-powered blender, blend the chickpeas, peanut butter, vanilla, baking powder, and salt (if desired) until smooth. 3. Using a spoon, mix in the chocolate chips. 4. Scoop out 1 tablespoon cookie dough and roll the scoop into a tight ball. Place the ball on the prepared baking sheet and flatten using your fingertips. Repeat until all the cookie dough is used. 5. Bake for 20 minutes or until the cookies turn golden brown.

Per Serving (2 cookies)

Calories: 302 | fat: 20g | protein: 9g | carbs: 27g | fiber: 5g

Pistachio Protein Ice Cream

Prep time: 25 minutes | Cook time: 0 minutes | Serves 8

1 can low-fat coconut milk
10 pitted Medjool dates
1 tablespoon vanilla extract
2 scoops organic pea protein
½ cup shelled pistachios

Optional Toppings:

Pomegranate seeds
Chopped dark chocolate
Fresh mint

1. Add all ingredients to a blender and blend into a smooth mixture. 2. Alternatively, add all ingredients to a medium bowl, cover it, and process using a handheld blender. 3. Freeze the mixture for 15 minutes, then stir it and freeze for another 10 minutes. 4. Add any desired toppings and freeze for at least 2 hours. 5. Store the ice cream in the freezer for a maximum of 90 days and thaw for 5 minutes at room temperature before serving.

Per Serving

Calories: 115 | fat: 4g | protein: 9g | carbs: 10g | fiber: 2g

Hippie Bonbons

Prep time: 10 minutes | Cook time: 0 minutes | Makes 19 bonbons

1½ cups Medjool dates, pitted
1 tablespoon fresh orange juice
1 teaspoon pure vanilla extract
½ teaspoon ground cinnamon
1 cup mixed raw nuts or seeds
½ teaspoon orange zest
½ teaspoon fine sea salt (optional)

1. In the bowl of a food processor, combine the pitted dates, nuts or seeds, orange juice, orange zest, vanilla, sea salt, if using, and cinnamon. Pulse the mixture a couple of times to chop everything. Then mix on high speed until the mixture sticks together and the nut pieces are quite small. 2. Scoop out a heaped tablespoon portion of the date and nut mixture, and roll the portion into a ball. Set the bonbon onto a dinner plate. Repeat with the remaining date and nut mixture. 3. The bonbons will keep in a sealed container in the refrigerator for about 1 week.

Per Serving (2 bonbons)

Calories: 104 | fat: 8g | protein: 3g | carbs: 7g | fiber: 2g

Basic Vanilla Chia Pudding

Prep time: 5 minutes | Cook time: 0 minutes | Serves 4

1 cup almond milk
⅓ cup chia seeds
1 teaspoon vanilla bean powder
½ cup full-fat coconut milk
1 tablespoon coconut sugar (optional)
Pinch of salt (optional)

1. Whisk all the ingredients together in a medium bowl. Stir every few minutes until thickened, about 15 minutes. Serve, or refrigerate for up to 48 hours.

Per Serving

Calories: 153 | fat: 14g | protein: 5g | carbs: 14g | fiber: 6g

Chapter 9 Staples, Sauces, Dips, and Dressings

Creamy Nut Sauce

Prep time: 15 minutes | Cook time: 20 minutes | Makes 2 cups

1 tablespoon extra-virgin coconut oil (optional)
3 large garlic cloves, finely chopped
1 tablespoon mirin
¼ cup filtered water
¾ cup boiling filtered water
1 medium onion, diced
½ teaspoon fine sea salt, plus more to taste (optional)
1 cup raw or toasted cashews, walnuts, or almonds
1 teaspoon tamari

1. Warm the oil in a medium skillet over medium-high heat. Add the onion and cook for 6 to 8 minutes, until golden. Stir in the garlic and salt, if using, and cook for 3 to 4 minutes, until the garlic is golden and fragrant. Add the mirin and the ¼ cup water, then raise the heat and bring to a simmer, stirring for a couple of minutes to deglaze the pan. 2. Remove from the heat and transfer the mixture to an upright blender, scraping the skillet with a rubber spatula. Add the nuts, boiling water, and tamari and blend until smooth, scraping the sides as necessary. Season to taste with more salt and serve immediately, or let cool and store in an airtight jar in the fridge for up to 4 days.

Per Serving (½ cup)

Calories: 188 | fat: 16g | protein: 4g | carbs: 9g | fiber: 2g

Savory Chia Crackers

Prep time: 20 minutes | Cook time: 20 minutes | Makes 36 crackers

½ cup oat flour
¼ cup water
1 teaspoon chia seeds
¼ teaspoon onion powder
½ cup brown rice flour
2 teaspoons nutritional yeast
¼ teaspoon freshly ground black pepper

1. Preheat the oven to 350°F (180°C). Cut 2 sheets of parchment paper the size of your baking sheet. Place them on a work surface. 2. In a food processor, combine the oat and brown rice flours, water, nutritional yeast, chia seeds, pepper, and onion powder. Process for 1 to 2 minutes to combine into a dough. You should be able to pinch the dough between two fingers without it sticking to you. 3. Place the dough on one of the sheets of parchment paper. Using your clean hands, press the dough together into a mound, then press to flatten and shape into a thick square. Place the other sheet of parchment paper on top. Using a rolling pin, evenly flatten the dough to ⅛ inch thick. If your dough is too thick, the crackers won't be crispy. Remove the top sheet of parchment paper and save it for another use. 4. Using a knife or pizza cutter, cut the dough into 36 (1-by-2-inch) rectangles. Using a fork, lightly prick holes in the center of each cracker. Carefully transfer the parchment paper with the dough on it to a baking sheet. 5. Bake for 10 minutes. Carefully flip the crackers and bake for 10 minutes more until golden brown on the edges. Transfer the crackers to a wire rack to cool. They will crisp as they cool. 6. Store in an airtight container at room temperature for up to 1 week or freeze for up to 1 month.

Per Serving (4 crackers)

Calories: 61 | fat: 1g | protein: 2g | carbs: 12g | fiber: 1g

Strawberry Chia Jam

Prep time: 2 minutes | Cook time: 10 minutes | Makes 1½ cups

3 cups frozen strawberries
¼ cup water
4 dates, pitted and chopped small
3 tablespoons chia seeds

1. In a medium saucepan over medium-high heat, combine the strawberries, dates, and water and bring to a boil. Lower the heat to medium-low and simmer, stirring occasionally, for 10 minutes. Remove from the heat.
2. Using a potato masher, mash the mixture until the jam is smooth but with some chunks remaining. Add the chia seeds and stir well. Transfer the mixture to a small jar, cover, and let cool. The jam will thicken as it cools. The jam can be stored in the refrigerator for up to 5 days.

Per Serving

Calories: 43 | fat: 1g | protein: 1g | carbs: 8g | fiber: 3g

Pineapple Salsa

Prep time: 5 minutes | Cook time: 0 minutes | Serves 8

1 pound (454 g) fresh or thawed frozen pineapple, finely diced, and juices reserved
1 jalapeño, minced (optional)
1 white or red onion, finely diced
1 bunch cilantro or mint, leaves only, chopped
Salt (optional)

1. Combine the pineapple with its juice, onion, cilantro, and jalapeño, if desired, in a medium bowl. Season with salt to taste and serve, if desired.

Per Serving

Calories: 40 | fat: 0g | protein: 0g | carbs: 10g | fiber: 1g

Roasted Bell Pepper Wedges

Prep time: 5 minutes | Cook time: 25 minutes | Makes 1½ cups

2 large red bell peppers, seeded and cut into wedges
Pinch freshly ground black pepper
½ teaspoon cumin seeds (optional)
1 tablespoon freshly squeezed lemon juice
½ teaspoon garlic powder (optional)

1. Preheat the oven to 425°F (220°C). 2. Place the bell pepper wedges in a large mixing bowl; then add the lemon juice, black pepper, garlic powder (if using), and cumin seeds (if using). Toss to combine. 3. Place the bell pepper wedges cut-side down on a baking sheet lined with nonstick foil or parchment paper. 4. Bake for 20 to 25 minutes until soft and lightly charred. Remove from the oven and cool for up to 20 minutes. Store in the refrigerator in an airtight container for up to 5 days.

Per Serving

Calories: 53 | fat: 1g | protein: 2g | carbs: 10g | fiber: 4g

Spicy Italian Vinaigrette

Prep time: 5 minutes | Cook time: 0 minutes | Makes 1 cup

1 cup apple cider vinegar
2 teaspoons maple syrup (optional)
¼ teaspoon salt (optional)
½ teaspoon garlic powder
½ cup extra-virgin olive oil (optional)
2 teaspoons Italian seasoning
¼ teaspoon black pepper
Pinch red pepper flakes

1. Combine the apple cider vinegar, olive oil, maple syrup, Italian seasoning, salt (if using), black pepper, garlic powder, and red pepper flakes in a jar, cover, and shake until well blended. The dressing can be stored in the refrigerator for up to 2 weeks.

Per Serving

Calories: 131 | fat: 14g | protein: 0g | carbs: 2g | fiber: 0g

BBQ Sauce

Prep time: 5 minutes | Cook time: 0 minutes | Serves 16

2 cups canned or fresh tomato cubes
3 tablespoons smoked paprika
2 tablespoons onion powder
5 pitted dates
2 tablespoons garlic powder

1. Add all the ingredients to a blender or food processor and blend to form a smooth sauce. 2. Store the BBQ sauce in the fridge, using an airtight container, and consume within 3 days. Alternatively, store it in the freezer for a maximum of 60 days and thaw at room temperature.

Per Serving

Calories: 11 | fat: 0g | protein: 0g | carbs: 2g | fiber: 0g

Beet Dressing

Prep time: 15 minutes | Cook time: 0 minutes | Makes 1 cup

1 small-medium cooked and cooled red beet
3 tablespoons raw cashew butter, coconut butter, or tahini
2 tablespoons extra-virgin olive oil (optional)
½ teaspoon fine sea salt, plus more to taste (optional)
¼ cup filtered water
2 tablespoons plus 1 teaspoon raw apple cider vinegar
1 (¼-inch) slice of a large garlic clove

1. Put the beet, water, nut or coconut butter or tahini, vinegar, olive oil, garlic, and salt, if using, in an upright blender and blend until completely smooth. Scrape down the sides with a rubber spatula and blend again. Adjust the seasoning to taste and blend again. 2. Serve immediately, or store in a glass jar in the fridge for up to 3 days. Shake well before using. The dressing will thicken once chilled; thin it out with a little water if needed.

Per Serving (¼ cup)

Calories: 141 | fat: 13g | protein: 3g | carbs: 6g | fiber: 1g

Lentil and Sweet Potato Bowl

Prep time: 25 minutes | Cook time: 30 minutes | Serves 4

Lentils:

3 tablespoons water
1½ teaspoons minced garlic
2 cups vegetable broth
½ cup diced red, white, or yellow onion
1 cup uncooked lentils, rinsed
1 teaspoon ground cumin

Base:

1 cup chopped kale, steamed
1 microwaved sweet potato, diced
1 cup cooked brown rice or quinoa

1. In a medium saucepan over medium-high heat, heat the water. Add the onion and garlic and sauté for 3 minutes or until the onion becomes tender and translucent. 2. Add the lentils, broth, and cumin and mix thoroughly. 3. Bring to a boil and mix until the bouillon cube is dissolved, 1 to 2 minutes. Cover and reduce the heat to low. Simmer for 20 minutes or until the lentils are soft. 4. Meanwhile, in a pot with a steamer basket, bring water to a boil over medium-high heat. Place the kale in the basket and steam for 3 to 4 minutes or until it softens. 5. Layer the rice (or quinoa), kale, lentils, and sweet potatoes in bowls.

Per Serving

Calories: 131 | fat: 1g | protein: 4g | carbs: 28g | fiber: 2g

Sour Cream

Prep time: 5 minutes | Cook time: 0 minutes | Serves 10

1 cup coconut cream
½ teaspoon apple cider vinegar
2 tablespoons lemon juice
½ teaspoon salt (optional)

1. Add all of the ingredients to a food processor or blender and blend until smooth. Alternatively, put all ingredients into a medium bowl and whisk using hand mixers until smooth. 2. Serve the sour cream chilled and enjoy as a topping or a side! 3. Store the sour cream in the fridge, using an airtight container, and consume within 4 days. Alternatively, store the sour cream in the freezer for a maximum of 60 days and thaw at room temperature.

Per Serving

Calories: 20 | fat: 1g | protein: 0g | carbs: 3g | fiber: 0g

Milton Keynes UK
Ingram Content Group UK Ltd.
UKHW050853241123
433162UK00004B/75